The John Grisham Story

For: Dixon Public Library

Libby Hughes

April 2005

The John Grisham Story

✦

From Baseball to Bestsellers

Libby Hughes

iUniverse, Inc.
New York Lincoln Shanghai

The John Grisham Story
From Baseball to Bestsellers

iUniverse, Inc.

For information address:
iUniverse, Inc.
2021 Pine Lake Road, Suite 100
Lincoln, NE 68512
www.iuniverse.com

Cover Photo: Rachel Zahumensky
Inside photos: Libby Hughes

ISBN: 0-595-32283-2

Printed in the United States of America

Dedicated to John Lloyd Hughes

Contents

ACKNOWLEDGMENTS

For the many people in Arkansas, Tennessee, and Mississippi, I want to express unlimited gratitude for their time and help in providing information for this book; especially to Billy Price Carroll in Memphis for her hospitality and chauffeuring abilities. Thomas Jones at the Memphis Library; Harriet Beeson and Corey Mesler at Burke's Bookstore; Evelyn Sims and LaVerne Davis at Southaven High School; Frances McGuffey; Barry Bouchillon; Linda G. Smith; Bobby and Shirley Grisham; Cheri at Blytheville Bookstore; Cynthia Williams; Professor Thomas K. Mason; Harry Randolph Garner; Parker Pickle; Carol Stubbs; Larry Little; Penny Pynkala; Carol Lamb; Dr. Linda Spargo; Mattie Sink; Jayne Buttross; Peggy Martin; Richard Howorth; Edward Perry; Billy Chadwick; Marc Smirnoff; Wanda Dean; Ron Polk; Dr. Nancy Hargrove; Dr. and Mrs. Lewis Sewell; Judge Toby Winston; Don Clanton; Sybil Huffstatter; Dr. Doris Herring; Dr. David Sansing; Dr. David Merritt; Margie Parks.

INTRODUCTION

Most writers and authors like to be invisible. They send their words into the universe to inspire and entertain. They wish the limelight to be upon their work and not on themselves. However, when publishers don't have the funds to promote an author's book, authors will make public appearances, grant interviews, and give speeches in their eagerness to sell books. In other words, they have to enter the marketing process—reluctantly.

For ten years after securing his law degree, John Grisham took center stage as a lawyer and politician, and he was successful. Both those careers disappointed him. He didn't like the seamy side of law, and it took too long to get things done in politics as a young legislator. But something he overheard in a Mississippi courtroom changed his life and his career. Grisham heard a ten-year-old black girl's testimony of being raped by two young white men. The horror of this tale compelled him to fictionalize this story. Every morning before he went to his law office, Grisham wrote for two hours. At the end of three years, he had written his first novel, *A Time to Kill.*

Grisham relished those early years of fame, but the constant invasion of privacy upon himself and his family became too excessive and wearing, forcing him to leave his beloved Oxford, Mississippi, and retreat to a secluded plantation in Charlottesville, Virginia.

Because of his aversion to reporters, the handsome Grisham became as secretive as Greta Garbo in "wanting to be alone." His closest friends and family dropped a protective cloak over his life.

Under these circumstances, this author set forth in her small van-camper with her two Rhodesian Ridgebacks to scour the landscape of Mississippi, Arkansas, and Tennessee to visit the various towns where Grisham lived and see the schools and universities he attended. Her research led her to family, teachers, professors, and friends, who were willing to share their remembrances.

The red clay of Mississippi and the rich, black delta of Arkansas painted many colorful scenes for the author and hopefully for the reader. By auditing law school classes at Ole Miss and pouring over archival material at Mississippi State University, the author was able to flesh out the mysterious portrait of the best-selling author, John Grisham.

Here is what she gleaned from her travels and research.

Libby Hughes
Cambridge, Massachusetts September, 2004

1

SHATTERED DREAMS OF BASEBALL FAME

Mississippi can have warm days and cool nights in March. It isn't winter and it isn't spring. The daffodils have poked their yellow heads through the earth. The Japanese magnolias are opening their pale pink blossoms. Rosebud trees begin to show their dark pink or pure white faces. A hint of sweet perfume is in the air. Herein lies the Mississippi mystique.

Every March, the baseball season is in full swing at Mississippi State University, located in Starkville, Mississippi. Baseball is what spring means to the students, residents, and fans nearby. By mid-February the empty bleachers begin to fill when the season opens. Trucks and trailers barrel down the highways to the heart of Mississippi. They bear northeast to the deserted plains of Starkville. They are going to Dudy Noble Field to grill, eat, and watch the college baseball games.

On one of those early March nights in 1975, a young man sat alone at the end of a bleacher close to first base. He wore a warm jacket to keep out the damp cold as he sipped from his thermos, filled with hot coffee, letting the steam bathe his face and warm his fingers. This was young John Grisham, a college student who had bounced around to different colleges in Mississippi and finally landed at MSU (Mississippi State University).

In his mind, Grisham could see the ball players take their positions and start the game. The floodlights would wash a white glow over Dudy Noble Field. He was in the shadows, but he could visualize the smoke, drifting across the field and into the stands from the grills in the Left Field Lounge. He could almost smell the charcoaled hamburgers, hot dogs, barbecued chicken, and spicy crayfish that always fill the air.

Food was the last thing on Grisham's mind. His stomach was in knots. He was not hungry. In fact, he was sad...very sad. As he imagined the players swinging their bats, he waited to hear the bat crack the ball and send it beyond the out-

1

field into a home run. When it happened, the crowd would be on its feet. They would yell. He knew the sound of the roar would echo down the slopes and through the dormitory windows in the distance. The happy player would lope slowly around the three bases, giving high-fives. The roar would climb again when he reached home plate. His team would embrace him, lift him, and slap him affectionately.

But John Grisham's heart was unmoved, frozen. His eyes watered slightly. He knew his dream would not come true. He would never be a famous baseball player. The crack on his bat would never be heard anywhere. That home run would never belong to him. The joyous roar from the crowd would never reach his ears. He swallowed the last of his coffee, slid off the bench, and went back to his apartment. What were the steps in coming to this agonizing decision?

◆　　　◆　　　◆

John Grisham had cherished his dream a long time. As a teenager, all sports were an obsession to him. In 1992 he told a reporter of "People Weekly," "I've always been real confident even in sports, where I had nothing to be confident about."

Being a professional football player was an early dream. But he soon realized he didn't have the physical build for the rough and tumble of the game. Even a quarterback needed more skill than he displayed. Okay, football was out. He had to reassess and decide to which sport he would devote his mind and body. He settled on baseball. Yes, he would do everything to become a professional baseball player.

Graduating from high school in 1973, Grisham looked around for a college that would fit his desire for a career in sports. Not far from his hometown of Southaven was Northwest Mississippi Junior College at Senatobia. The rural town with its wide-open spaces and white sycamore trees was perfect for the young baseball enthusiast. He promptly entered and played there for a year. His studies were secondary to his baseball passion.

Soon, though, he became restless. Northwest was not a challenge and he decided to transfer to Delta State University in the small town of Cleveland, Mississippi. Delta State had the one thing he wanted…a famous head baseball coach. This was Dave Ferriss.

Ferriss had made it in the big leagues. He had started out at MSU and distinguished himself as a college player in the 1940s. Before long, Ferriss was signed to the Boston Red Sox as a pitcher. In 1946 the Red Sox made it to the American

League pennant and he won the Cy Young Award as a result. Through the years, Ferriss served as Boston's pitching coach and finally, he returned to his Mississippi roots. Delta State tapped him for their athletic director and head baseball coach. If Ferriss could make it, so could John Grisham from Southaven, Mississippi. The country heard about Ferriss, why couldn't they hear about Grisham?

When John Grisham first strode out to the plate with his bat, he was sure this was only the beginning of his career under Ferriss' guidance. Greatness in the World Series was somewhere in the near future. All went well at Delta State for the first three weeks. Then he faced reality.

"One day," said Grisham, "I stood at home plate and watched in horror as a fastball came directly at my head at 90 miles per hour. It missed, but I was sick at my stomach. The next pitch was a bit slower, but nonetheless, headed straight for my ear. I immediately dived toward the third base and did not see the ball as it dropped and curved beautifully across the plate. I heard laughter as I rolled in the din and grass. I faked back spasms and crawled to the dugout. The next day, 'Boo' Ferriss, the perfect gentleman, called me into his office and confessed he didn't think I could hit a fastball. And, since it had already been established I couldn't hit a curve, there wasn't much left. Pitchers can be cruel when they spot weaknesses."

The fascination with Delta State University quickly faded. Although still in denial about his baseball prowess, Grisham and his roommates decided it was time to move on and try a third university. They were all restless. Mississippi State University wasn't too far away. Just across the state about 100 miles. And so, as a sophomore, John Grisham transferred yet again.

That March night in the baseball bleachers at MSU was a turning point for the nomadic Grisham. He had come to the realization that baseball would not be in the cards for him as a way to earn a living. His mind, not his heart, told him the Baseball Hall of Fame would not be citing him as one of America's all time greats. Even though his dreams about professional baseball were shattered, it did not mean the sport would drop completely out of his life. His obsession would channel him into a devoted spectator of local, college, and national games. Also, as a married man, he would turn his energies into becoming a coach for Little League. In reality, John Grisham reluctantly faced the fact that he would have to live out his dream in a different form.

Little did he know in those transient college days that fame, applause, and autograph-seekers would surround him in the future. Grisham would hit home run after home run on "The New York Times" bestseller list, defeating some of his outstanding rivals in the field of legal, suspense books.

How, then, did this failed baseball player transform his obscure life from a poor cotton farm in Arkansas to a best-selling author from Mississippi and Virginia? And would wealth and fame bring him happiness? Would celebrity and money corrupt him or would life bring him fulfillment? These were burning questions that could be posed to anyone who seeks and finds success.

2

A POOR RURAL
CHILDHOOD

Mississippi is not a very big state. It is caught in the throat of the deep South and looks like a chunky-heeled boot, ready to walk westward. On the east, its cheek borders Alabama. On its west cheek stretches Arkansas and Louisiana. Above its head is Tennessee. Under its foot washes the warm, jade-green waters of the Gulf of Mexico beyond the barrier reefs.

Memphis, Tennessee, adopted home of Elvis Presley (Elvis was actually born and raised in Tupelo, Mississippi), rests on the hairline of Mississippi. Memphis stares across the Mississippi River to the banks of Arkansas and looks down its nose to Mississippi.

Across the bridge, Arkansas fans into long flat stretches of cotton fields. Driving 60 miles northwest from Memphis sits Jonesboro, Arkansas, on Crowley's Ridge. In the 1950s Jonesboro was a slow, small town of 12,000 to 18,000 people. Today, it approaches 50,000. Farming and light industry was the heart of its working force. There were 37 cotton gins and two rice mills.

For rural communities, the closest hospital was in Jonesboro. When it came time for Wanda and John Grisham, Sr., to have their second of five children, they drove from Black Oak, Arkansas, to Jonesboro. On February 8, 1955 John Grisham, Jr. was born. John would be the first of three sons and they were very happy to celebrate his birth.

The parents of John Grisham had grown up in Arkansas. Wanda Skidmore (his mother) grew up in Black Oak. According to folks in the area, Wanda's mother was a very sweet woman. She had red hair and bright blue eyes. Her father sold pianos in nearby communities. Wanda herself was musical and played the piano. John Grisham, Sr., came from Booneville, Arkansas. He was one of five brothers. From Booneville, they lived in Lake City, Arkansas, where some of the brothers worked at the cotton gin. In fact, some of the relatives claim that seven Grisham brothers came over on the Mayflower in 1620 and scattered across the country, changing the spelling of the Grisham name to Grissom.

Black Oak is hardly a speck on the map and could be missed by passing a bend in the road or the blink of an eye. It could be gone in seconds. But the tiny town is there, surrounded by bobbing heads of white cotton blossoms and fields of soybeans. Only two hundred people live in Black Oak. Perhaps there were even fewer people in 1955. Many of them were Grisham relatives. Families represent the soul of the South. Sometimes there are feuds and sometimes there aren't, but blood is definitely thicker than water.

The main street in Black Oak is sparse and not too long. In late summer and early fall, the wind-blown clumps of cotton fly across the street and hug the curbs. The Cafe (now Vera's Cafe) is still the favorite place to gather for breakfast, lunch, and gossip. Weathered gray planks cover the outside. Inside, oilcloth, checkered tablecloths cling to the wooden tables. The smell of grits, fried chicken, catfish, okra, black-eyed peas, and cornbread flow from the open kitchen. The customers watch the waitresses balance a pile of plates and wait to be served as they exchange bits of humor with neighbors and sweet-talking waitresses. The grocery store is only steps away. A small post office is across the road. Down the street is the Baptist Church, which represents the center of life for most southern towns.

When Wanda and John were first married, they lived in Black Oak. Their house had only four rooms and was made of plank boards. It had no indoor plumbing. Trees and a cotton field surrounded the house, which Big John owned. They were poor, but happy. When the house became too small for their growing family, Big John bought a white house two miles away near the highway. It had three bedrooms and indoor plumbing. Trees kept the house shaded during the hot summers. The young couple and their small children were glad to move there.

Among Big John's relatives were a nephew, Bobby Grisham, and his wife Shirley. Wanda and Shirley were friends and lived only a short distance apart. With small babies and toddlers, they occasionally did some baby-sitting for each other.

"I remember one time Wanda left Little John with me while she went to the doctor," said Shirley Grisham. "Before she left, we were laughing over something and baby John fell accidentally on the floor. All of Wanda's children were mad. They thought their Mama had hurt the baby. The Grisham children were real close siblings."

Shirley recalled that John Grisham as a child was quiet and shy, but loved to play sports even at a young age. All his brothers and sisters played in the yard outside their small wooden house. The cotton bushes of the farm stretched as far as they could see. Little John would spend hours picking cotton under the hot sun.

Wanda and Big John were a traditional, married couple in the sense that they were the product of the 1950s. Wanda looked after the house and children. Big John went out and worked to provide a living for his wife and family. He was considered the boss. That's what Wanda wanted and expected from her husband. She was in charge of the children, and there were two things Wanda demanded of them. They had to go to the Baptist church and they had to get a library card to read books. Whenever they moved to a new town, Wanda took the children to the church and library before anything else.

"We didn't have a lot of money," John Jr. said, "but we didn't know it. We were well-fed and loved and scrubbed."

At the dinner table, the Grisham family said grace as an expression of thanks to God for their food and blessings. Most households in the South follow this tradition. Children were expected to offer the blessing when asked by their parents. Wanda, John, and their children attended the First Baptist Church in Black Oak twice on Sundays and usually slid into the front row pew. The Grisham children were always quiet and wellmannered.

According to friends and relatives, Wanda Grisham had a good-natured and lovable disposition. She did not like or permit the use of bad language by her children at home or in public. Her nephew, Bobby Grisham, said of her, "Wanda is one of the sweetest people in the world you'll ever meet." According to Bobby, Wanda is very pretty as well. He described Big John as a blustery, generous, and nice-looking man, full of stories to tell. But also, he was strict and a strong disciplinarian, making his children a little afraid of him.

When it came time for school, little John was sent down the highway to Monette for elementary school. The glass and pale yellow brick, one-storied building faced the busy highway between acres and acres of cotton-fields. Everything was flat, dry, and dusty. In Kindergarten and first grade, little John sat quietly behind his small wooden desk. He would spend only one or two semesters there.

To support his wife and five children, Big John Grisham had to find jobs on construction sites or work a dragline on the levees. There was too much competition in cotton farming. So, Big John and Wanda left the close relatives and friends in Black Oak to begin crisscrossing Arkansas, Louisiana, and Mississippi, working for a busy construction company. Wanda and the children followed Big John wherever the work was. The family would pick up their belongings and go to the next town or state. Wanda never complained. Her job was to make a happy home.

Southeast of Black Oak was a small town in Mississippi called Crenshaw. With less than a thousand people in the town, Big John and Wanda Grisham moved there with their children. Crenshaw was one of those Delta towns, divided by the Illinois Central Railroad. White people lived on one side of the tracks and black people on the other side. Today, the racial lines don't exist and Crenshaw elects African-American mayors.

The northern part of Crenshaw is hilly with sandy-colored earth. Below the hills, is the rich, black soil of the Delta. Cotton, beans, and corn grow in abundance. Large plantations spread their fields across the Delta land in the old days. The white landowners hired the black people to plant and pick the harvest alongside the nearby Cold Water River—a tributary to the larger Yazoo River. In the early days, many of the homes were built near the railroad. Even the grandson of the founder, Dr. Crenshaw, still lives there. Only 35 miles from Memphis, the residents of Crenshaw looked to that major Tennessee city for entertainment, newspapers, and medical facilities. Today, they can look to larger Mississippi towns for these needs.

For the Grishams, Crenshaw was another sleepy town, providing construction work for Big John. As long as Wanda could join a Baptist church and get library cards for her children, she was content.

From Crenshaw, Big John's company moved him south to Delhi, Louisiana, where the population was at least 10,000. Essentially Delhi was an agricultural town. However, the oil and gas industry began to grow after World War II. Because the Bayou Macon was connected to the Mississippi River, trade by steamships was used until the Vicksburg and Shreveport Railroad came through the heart of Delhi. It was a vital transportation point for sending confederate soldiers to Vicksburg, Mississippi, during the Civil War. Delhi still maintains an original soda fountain in its drugstore for selling sodas and ice cream as they were served in times past.

Louisiana is a state with an air of mystery. The swamps are eerie when the broken Cypress trees rise out of the black, murky waters. The large warts around the base of the trees look like human knees. In the orange light of sunset, the smooth trunks are dark and mysterious. They look like something out of Stephen King's stories where malformed creatures come to life.

Delhi, too, has a fascinating history. Two brothers, Frank and Jesse James were famous outlaws. They robbed from the rich and gave to the poor and to themselves. They had friends and relatives in Delhi and stopped there during their travels on horseback. One time a widow, who owed $700, told the James brothers about her debt. They gave her the money and then robbed the man after he collected it from her!

Even the name of the town has a romantic twist to it. In the middle 1800s, there weren't any formal schools for children. A young man was hired as a tutor and taught the offspring of a number of families around Delhi. He read oriental stories in verse by Thomas Moore. "Lallah Rookh," one of the tales, told about the daughter of the emperor of Delhi, India, who fell in love with a traveling young man. The tutor underlined the word "Delhi" throughout the book. One day he rode into town to the railroad junction and carved "Delhi" into the bark of a large oak tree. When the train arrived, the conductor saw the name and called the railroad stop "Delhi." From that time, the town had its name.

When young John Grisham became a successful writer, he wrote a book called "The Pelican Brief." In it, he uncovers a plot to destroy the pelican wildlife in a Louisiana area for the purpose of setting up oil and gas rigs. In his book "The Testament" he mentions the town of Delhi. Whatever little John Grisham remembered about Louisiana and Delhi, he pulled from his memory and fed it into his novel.

Soon, the Grisham family moved again. This time to Parkin, Arkansas, which is 60 miles southeast of Jonesboro. Parkin is located on the St. Francis River and had a population less than 1,800 when the Grishams lived there. Its fame comes from the Parkin Archeological State Park where Indian villages date back to the 1500s. The area covers 17 acres. The Spanish explorer, Hernando De Soto, visited Parkin in the summer of 1541. De Soto went all over the south and many southern states have counties and parks named after him.

Along the river are ceremonial mounds of dirt like small pyramids, but with flat tops. Temples could have been built on the mounds and sometimes houses for chiefs or important people in the village. The archaeologists called the people Mississippians. They were farmers who raised corn, beans, and squash. Fish-hooks, bones, and pottery pieces have been found to prove their existence. Obviously, the people fished from the banks of the river.

While Big John worked seven days on construction, something very special happened to little John at the age of eight. He had a religious conversion.

In an interview with "Christianity Today" in 1994, John Grisham told about this incident. "I came under conviction when I was in third grade, and I talked with my mother. I told her, 'I don't understand this, but I need to talk to you.' We talked and she led me to Jesus. The following Sunday I made a public confirmation of my faith. In one sense, it was not terribly eventful for an eight-year-old, but it was the most important event in my life. It did not readily change me, but it was very real nonetheless."

Within a year or two the Grishams moved again. Big John's construction company sent him over to Mississippi again. This time they went to Ripley, Mississippi, southeast of Memphis. The population would approach 5,000 by the 1990s. When the Grisham family arrived there in the 1960s, it was probably half that number.

Ripley, too, was soaked in adventurous history. The town was named after Wheelock Ripley, who was a hero in the war of 1812 and a Congressman. Since 1893 the town has run a huge flea market every Monday, which spreads over five acres and draws thousands to its stalls.

A colorful character named Colonel William Faulkner (great grandfather to the famous writer, William Faulkner of Oxford, Mississippi) came to Ripley in 1837. His favorite uncle was put in jail for a murder that took place just outside Ripley. Colonel Faulkner had to walk to and from the prison and vowed that he would one day build a railroad. When he actually built it, the Colonel became a local hero. In 1880 the Colonel also wrote a novel called, "The White Roads of Memphis." Perhaps his great-grandson inherited that gift for writing. Colonel Faulkner also was elected to Congress. Ironically, when he ran for reelection, he was shot and killed on the streets of Ripley.

By the time young John and his siblings reached Ripley, they would experience a more stable school life. Their father wasn't moving as frequently.

A sixth grade classmate, Sherril Mauney McCoy, from Ripley recalled John Grisham as good-looking, an athlete, a good sport, and real smart. "None of us thought we'd be famous, but we're proud of him. I can tell you that."

From an elementary school graduation yearbook, Barbara Smith Graddy could point to pictures of herself as the queen and John as the king of Ripley Elementary. She remembered him as "just a normal kid. A quick wit, that's what made him stand out. He could be sarcastic, quick on retort, had a comeback for everything. Like all kids that age we were interested in sports and cheer-leading, things like that."

When John's mother Wanda was asked about her son, she said, "He always read a lot. I don't remember him writing, but he was always able to express himself well. He was a pretty wellrounded kid, played sports, was in Scouts for a while, active in church. It was a normal childhood, growing up in a house full of kids, the oldest son. He was dependable, took the lead, but a very average kid. And yes, he got into some meanness now and then."

Yet, the very fact of moving from one town and one state to the next would be beneficial to John Grisham as a writer. When asked about this kind of life as a child, he said, "Though we moved around like gypsies, it was a lot of fun."

Most southerners love to talk and tell stories whether they are at a party, around the dinner table, or on the telephone. John Grisham confirmed this attribute with reference to his family. "My father's family is a family of storytellers, and there were long dinners and lots of stories. As children, we absorbed them."

What was John Grisham like as a teenager and as a college student? Even as a teen, he had the beginnings of movie star good looks, but there remained a quiet mystery about him. Where would these qualities take him?

3

MISSISSIPPI ROOTS
GO DEEP

The gypsy life of the Grisham family would soon come to an end. With five children in school, Wanda and Big John Grisham decided to put down roots in Mississippi. Work was plentiful. They liked the people in this Mississippi town, finding them warm and hospitable. Their children liked it, too, and when they moved from Ripley to Southaven in 1967, it felt like home. Wanda was ready to have her children in one place where they could have friends and could grow up in a good Baptist church.

Southhaven is at the "Top of Mississippi." The suburbs of Memphis, Tennessee, sprawl into Arkansas and Mississippi. Going south from Memphis, Southhaven is 25 miles on the southern flank of bumpy flatland. The rich, red clay earth, plowed and leveled, continues to await the building of more new homes and businesses.

In the 1960s and even today, families could afford homes and could afford the property taxes in Southaven. Crime wasn't a problem like it was in Memphis. The pace was slower and friendlier. The most notable piece of history about Southaven, aside from John Grisham, is its cemetery where soldiers from the Civil War were buried.

Otherwise, everything feels new. Gas stations are on every corner. Familiar fast food restaurants can be seen everywhere. Residential areas are private, but handy to businesses and shops. Trees are not in abundance because of the growth spurt. When the Grishams moved there, the American Electric Company had erected a 130-foot water tower. It looked like a huge golf ball sitting on a golf tee, causing many humorous comments.

Whitehaven was a closer suburb to Memphis. Not knowing what to name the new little town, they simply called it "Southaven" because it was south of Whitehaven. Furthermore, Southaven was squeezed between two other suburbs—Olive Branch and Horn Lake, which were older, more established towns.

The Grishams settled happily into Southaven. Big John ran a dealership for heavy farm equipment while Wanda became involved in the First Baptist Church and looked after the needs of Beth, little John, Kenny, Mark, and Wendy—her five children. They were able to establish long-lasting friendships and gain a sense of community, which was Wanda's desire for all of them.

When John was 14 or 15 and still at Horn Lake High School (two miles from his home), he and his friends couldn't wait for Saturday mornings. Unlike most teenagers, they didn't want to sleep on Saturday mornings. Instead, they gathered together and awakened their sports coach to ask for the key to the gymnasium. Playing basketball all day Saturday was their passion. For lunch everybody went to the store for hamburgers and fries. Sometimes, they played the pinball machines, but then, it was back to the basketball court for the afternoon.

One of the team players remembered how young John Grisham had a fancy way of dribbling the ball behind him. All the players were in awe of him, except one. He was the only African-American in the group. He was fast. He was like lightning. His job was to guard John Grisham. As John began to dribble the ball behind him, the guard whipped behind him, captured the ball, and scored a basket. A look of surprise and disbelief stole across Grisham's face. He had been outdone.

When the boys weren't playing inside the gym, they played basketball on the street, in driveways, or on patios where there were basketball backboards and nets.

Because Southaven didn't have a high school until 1971, little John still had to attend the one in Horn Lake, which was overcrowded. Some of the classes had to be held in neighboring churches. In fact, the gymnasium was used as both a library and a stage. Once Southaven High School was finished in 1971, little John transferred for his junior and senior years. He couldn't have been happier. The Grisham house at 1230 Coventry Cove was only minutes from the new red-brick school with its tall pillars at the entrance on Rasco Drive.

Inside the new high school, everything was gleaming. The linoleum floors were shiny and the corridors wide. The concrete block walls were snow-white. At the top of all the halls, stripes of red and blue were bright and patriotic.

But little John Grisham focused on his passion at Southaven High—football and baseball. His coach, Don Clanton, later Superintendent of Schools in Senatobia, Mississippi, remembered young John Grisham well. "He was a great kid and had leadership abilities. But I never thought of him as a writer. Although he was good at football, he had no speed. In those days, he was a bit chunkier. He was willing to play any position, but just too slow. As far as baseball, he was a fair player. He had all the right work ethics and came to all the practices. He had a good personality. And he was an outstanding citizen. One other thing, John was never too busy to forget where he came from."

With his sports obsession, John's studies didn't receive the same attention. One of his eleventh grade teachers, Miss Sims, had some vivid recollections. She taught "Survey of American Literature." The attractive, blonde teacher was a young mother in 1971. She was petite and full of sweet femininity.

"In class John was an average student...he chose to be. His interests were diverse," she said. "He was more into sports. He was a good writer. He wrote some original poetry and short stories. Had a gift for writing. He was perceptive about people. His observations were insightful. He was straightforward...almost clipped. There was a kind of cynicism...he didn't take things at face value. He asked probing questions. He seemed more mature than his peers. Although not an enthusiastic student, he did make 'B's.' He was never a disciplinary problem and he had supportive parents."

Then, Mrs. Sims smiled. "He was voted one among five young men who had a handsome appearance. He had a good personality, but he could see things in people that others missed. He was not overly impressed by anything...not flashy, not superficial. John had the respect of his peers. There was a dignity about him that was admirable. He had definite ideas about what was right and wrong. And he wasn't cliquish and not a loner. Though he wasn't a joiner, he wasn't exclusive."

Mrs. Sims walked down a long corridor and pointed to a corner wall. At the top were photos of the graduating class from 1973. There, between two pretty blonde girls was a round-faced John Grisham, wearing a bow tie. His hair fell low over his forehead and a slight smile hovered on his lips.

Another English teacher at Southaven High School had a profound effect on Grisham. She was Frances McGuffey, who taught senior English to John. Her class introduced him to books and authors that captured his interest. One of them was California novelist and short story writer, John Steinbeck, who portrayed the tragic life of poor migrant workers in the 1939 novel, *Grapes of Wrath.*" These people were the"Okies," who traveled to California in broken down trucks, looking for work and money in California, but were bitterly disappointed. Steinbeck won a Pulitzer Prize for this book. Actor Henry Fonda made the story memorable in the movie version.

"John liked the writer John Steinbeck; especially his book *Tortilla Flat*," said Mrs. McGuffey. "He liked comparing authors, but I missed any interest he himself might have had in writing."

This 1935 Steinbeck novel was his fourth. Set in the 1920s, *Tortilla Flat* portrays the life of Hispanic/American Indians, known as pasianos. They lived on the flat (flat as a tortilla), dusty, poor, township outside the affluent town of Monterey, California. There are seventeen episodes, shifting quickly from one to the next. John Grisham has many episodes and subplots in his own novels. Steinbeck had little character development. Like the Steinbeck novels, the first three Grisham novels had little character exploration. Relationships are more important than material things in the Steinbeck novels. Perhaps, Grisham related to the migrant lives of these workers. His childhood had been full of moves from place to place.

These similarities between Steinbeck and Grisham were not apparent to Mrs. McGuffey in her senior English class. But she was very aware of the personal aspects of John Grisham as a teenager. "He had a dry sense of humor although he was serious and an athlete. He was a cutup, but wholesome, nice, and a hard worker. He would hire his sister to make his bed for him and pay her 25 cents. The Grisham children tried to outdo each other. And their Dad would kill them if they didn't do the right thing. His mother, Wanda, was a quiet pillar of strength. Mrs. Grisham never forced her children to do things. She did it with gentleness. She had their respect."

Mrs. McGuffey made more observations about her student, John Grisham. "He was always a gentleman. Never took advantage of others. He was good-humored and a sense of integrity and honor. He never cheated," she said. "Home ties interest him. John always asks about so and so and how he's doing. He is kind and never forgets friends. When speaking to Southaven students, he has told them to do things with their lives. They asked him if he would go back to practicing law. He said that if he had to shave and wear socks, he wouldn't."

"In fact," said McGuffey, "he was disillusioned as a legislator and found himself so busy that he didn't have time to watch his children grow up. Family means the most to him. When he started writing full time at home, his son thought his Dad had lost his job."

John Grisham had his own recollections of his teacher and how she inspired him to read books. "The first book I remember that really grabbed me was a book that Mrs. McGuffey made us read, a book called *Tortilla Flat* by Steinbeck. And when I read it, I really enjoyed the book. And so I went to her and said, 'This is really good. I like this.' And she was shocked that I would show any interest in what she was making us do. So she said, okay, read this. And the next one was *Of Mice and Men*. So she sort of fed the Steinbeck books to me. When I read *The Grapes of Wrath*—we saved that for last—I knew that was a very powerful book. And I don't know if it had anything to do with my writing style, or me as a writer, because I wasn't thinking about it back then. It had a lot to do with the way I viewed humanity and the struggles of little people against big people. It was a very important book for me."

Grisham further remembered, "Once I had gone through all of Steinbeck's books, I realized that I had had a wonderful experience. I remember thinking, 'I'd love to be able to write this clearly.' At the same time we were having to read Faulkner. So we had Faulkner on the one hand, and Steinbeck on the other, and Steinbeck looked remarkably clear, compared to Faulkner."

When the Grisham children weren't involved in school and sports, they took part in church activities. The family joined the First Baptist Church of Southaven shortly after their move in 1967. Later, they would join the Carriage Hills Baptist Church in their residential neighborhood.

Some family friends, LaVerne and Gerald Davis, were also members of the same church. The husband-wife team taught the College and Career Group for ages 19 to 22.

LaVerne Davis, while working in Southaven's high school office, recalled those youthful days in teaching John Grisham. "They were good boys, but boys," she said. "They discussed the Bible School lessons. And the Church had a service project...to visit a nursing home once a month. I remember one incident. I'm someone known for getting the giggles and not being able to stop. I was in a room seeing patients when I heard an echo from the hall, 'LaVerne, come help me.' When I went out, there were three boys...John, being one. Then, I got the giggles. Those boys had a ball laughing at me. They loved picking on me. Well, I was a neighbor to the Grishams and my kids grew up with their kids."

Mrs. Davis started to laugh and said, "I remember a camping trip up the Tennessee River. John and the other boys took an army tent and set it up on this island. Well, it rained and rained. The water even crept under the tent. While we tried to sleep through the wet night, John and another boy got away and slept in the cars. He was always playing pranks."

A broad grin spread across her face, "I wasn't surprised that John became a writer because he told such tall tales and you believed them."

Her reflections became more serious. "John's a very loyal friend and he helps members of his family. When his sister's husband needed a transplant, John paid all the expenses," she said. "His parents are from the old school. The husband is the head of the household. They were always together at church. But when Wanda was pregnant, Big John didn't want her to be seen in public. His mother is so sweet and attractive. The two Johns were called Big John and Little John."

Soon high school days would be over for young Grisham. In June of 1973, young John would stride across the auditorium stage to receive his diploma from Southaven High School. Not knowing what he wanted to do—except play baseball, John drifted for a year to Northwest Mississippi Community College. Here he flunked a freshman course in English. Then he spent a semester at Delta State. Both colleges had baseball teams and he was drawn to them for that reason. When it became apparent he did not meet the standard, he looked for another university.

Would the third university give him some direction and some purpose?

4

FROM PARTY BOY TO
SERIOUS STUDENT

John Grisham's next stop would be on the rumpled, sandy plains of northeast Mississippi at Starkville. Once a sawmill town, surrounded by cotton plantations, Starkville now claims to be home for Mississippi State University. Its nearest city is Columbus, which bumps the border of Alabama. Columbus was hometown to famous playwright, Tennessee (Tom) Williams.

The highways from Alabama through Mississippi bypass Starkville and serve as a thoroughfare to a continuous convoy of heavy trucks. They travel east and west whether day or night, going from coast to coast. The droning, pounding, and deep-throated horns are unheard by the students on campus. They were oblivious of the commercial life outside their campus dormitories, classrooms, and playing fields. MSU was a world to itself.

The campus terrain sprawls over 4,200 acres. It is both flat and hilly. The slopes are uneven and creased. The highest point is the football stadium, which dominates the whole campus. On its flank is the Dudy Noble baseball field while classroom and dormitory buildings spread out on the far side of the football field's apron. Historically, the college began as Mississippi A & M (Agriculture and Mechanical) in 1878. Today it still specializes in agriculture and engineering. For that reason, the university is nicknamed "The People's College." Its long history has brought a mixture of architecture from the Beaux Arts period as reflected by Lee Hall in the 1900s to the sleek modern lines of McCool Hall.

After the football stadium, the Drill Field is the next focal point. The Drill Field is the long quadrangle that reaches from Lee Hall to the Mitchell Memorial Library. Sidewalks crisscross the quad amid statues. Originally, freshmen and sophomores were required to take ROTC. At noon every day, the students, strolling to and from classes or breaking for lunch, watched the marching cadet officers. Thus the name, Drill Field, still remains. ROTC is no longer required, so the marching only occurs occasionally.

Yet, Mississippi State University shines with the brilliance of floral beauty in the early spring. In sunny corners, the Japanese magnolias open their blossoms in delicate pink and cream colors. They soften the harshness of winter and suggest the loveliness of the South. Although the magnolia is the state flower, the Japanese magnolia is slightly smaller and more fragile in appearance. By May, the large crepe myrtle shrubs burst into bloom with thick clusters of deep pink and rose-colored petals. The students often feel as if they are walking through an Impressionist painting. By late fall, the maple trees have turned a tawny yellow and rusty red.

Into this colorful display John Grisham arrived among 10,000 other students in 1975. He came with an attitude of arrogance, which he remembers with humor. In Mississippi State's 1991 "Alumnus" Magazine, Grisham describes this episode.

"I was a sophomore, I think. The uncertainty is because I had transferred around so much and lost so many hours that no one could determine exactly my status. I had also changed majors three times in three semesters, and this contributed heavily to the confusion. In fact, I arrived on campus unannounced, unregistered, without transcripts, and generally unconcerned by any of this. After all, I was just passing through. I had two roommates and we were in the process of sampling every college in the state. My parents were paying for this, and even they had lost track of where I happened to be enrolled."

He continued in the article, "And so it came to pass that I stood with an attitude before a very patient lady in the admissions office and listened as she explained why I could not be admitted until my transcripts arrived. I had no idea where my transcripts were, I said rudely, and furthermore, I really didn't care. If State didn't want me, I'd simply go elsewhere. We'd been in Starkville three days, and my roommates were already restless."

Making a joke about himself and praising the lady who didn't react, Grisham wrote, "She was a pro at handling jerks, and after huddling with her superior it was determined I could take classes for a few days until my records arrived. I wrote a check for the tuition and fees, and a week later this same sweet lady called my apartment and informed me the check had bounced. I had arrived."

Supposing that lady had refused to enroll John Grisham. What would have been his career path? Would he have become the successful writer we have today? Or would he have become a directionless drifter? We will never know the answer to that hypothetical question. Perhaps Grisham and his readers owe this woman in the admissions office a debt of gratitude.

Thus began the transformation of 20-year-old John Grisham from a serial party boy to a serious student.

In this same article, Grisham reflected on an incident that had a profound effect on his life and study habits. "In the course of all this, I had changed my major to finance, I think, and my classes were in Bowen Hall. McCool Hall was not yet finished. Attending classes was a new experience for me. My first one was some species of economics. The instructor was a crusty old fellow who, on the first day, made the mistake of suggesting the military should step in and protect Saigon, South Vietnam, during the evacuation of American troops at the end of the Vietnam War. This was 1975, when the communists were still rampaging, and our part of the war had been over for two years. This professor was one of those conservative bomb throwers who thought war was fine as long as someone else was fighting it, and his big mistake was to spout his beliefs before a class which happened to include two Vietnam veterans, one of whom had been wounded and neither of whom appreciated his armchair strategies. A vicious debate erupted as these veterans took him to task and virtually stripped him naked before the class. He tried to hold his ground, but he was rather pitiful. Others smelled blood, and he was soon surrounded by a nasty pack of angry students. It was wonderful. I was amazed at my classmates who were articulate and prepared and unafraid of attacking a Professor."

This incident was a landmark in Grisham's academic life. He continued to relate its impact in the article. "Of course, I contributed nothing to the discussion. I hadn't even purchased the textbook. But at that moment, in my first class at State, I became a student—not a radical, but a kid who suddenly wanted to grow up and learn. I wanted to be able to attack professors and tie them in knots with my deft arguments and piercing analyses."

"I bought the textbook, and went to the class for two weeks before dropping it. Economics was not my bag. One of the veterans was an accounting major with impeccable grades. He was bitter about the war, and he wanted to go to law school so he could sue people and in general fight the system. My grades were far from impeccable, but they were salvageable, he thought, but only if I went to work. He said that accounting was the toughest major in business, and if I couldn't get into law school I would still have an excellent degree."

"Much to the amazement of my roommates, I began to study and attend classes. I took notes, read the assignments, wrote the papers, and prepared for the exams. I decided it was best not to attack professors because, as I quickly learned, these guys give the grades, and suddenly I was caught up in the competition for grades. I laid off the professors. Lucky for them. By mid-term of that first semester, I was a regular scholar. We moved into McCool Hall, and I was there bright and early every morning reading the Wall Street Journal and brushing up on the assignments. I decided I would specialize in tax law and make millions representing rich people."

"By the end of the semester, my roommates were ready to move on. They had watched my transformation with much suspicion, and it was time for the moment of truth. They announced they were leaving State and demanded to know if I would leave with them. No, I said. I had found a home. Our journey was over. We parted as good friends, and remain so to this day."

And so, John Grisham began a new chapter in his life…that of a student, a serious student, a student who had a purpose.

However, he had one roommate left. He was James Parker Pickle from Love, Mississippi, not far from John's home in Southaven. They had met through friends and had shared an apartment with two others at Delta State for that one semester. Once they had found an apartment near MSU, they set up bachelor housekeeping.

Parker was a handsome young man with a dazzling smile…almost like Donny Osmond's. An expert basketball player, he enjoyed playing with John and outwitting him. "John fathomed he could beat me at basketball," said Parker in a soft southern drawl, "but he never did."

"We learned about bill paying, cooking, and cleaning. John loved to cook spaghetti," recalled Parker. "He was a great roommate…conscientious and funny. He was very private and standoffish. He was studious in school and good at sports and got good grades. He liked to discuss literature and drama. Yet, he read *MAD* magazine. English, literature, and reading were his favorite pastimes. He turned to business and law because he couldn't make a living as a writer."

Parker Pickle came from a large family of eight children. His parents had a dairy farm, which John Grisham enjoyed visiting. "He loved my mother, 'Gran.' She was a wonderful cook. He even mentioned Mrs. Pickle's cat in *A Time to Kill*. He sent her a signed copy of every one of his books. When she was ill for eight years, he always found time to write her and send a first edition," said Parker.

Today, Parker Pickle is tax assessor for De Soto County in Mississippi. He works in the De Soto County Courthouse, which Grisham used as his model in *A Time to Kill*.

Meanwhile, John spent most of his time going to classes in the new McCool Hall with its red brick facade and tall, skinny columns. Sometimes, he sat outside on the steps, watching the pretty young women students walking by. But most of the time he was inside slogging through the courses he needed for a B.S. degree in accountancy.

One of these courses was "Cost Accountancy" given by Dr. Dora Herring. This was a course for those interested in being managers of a company. It was required.

"John was quiet and sat on the back row. He didn't like the subject because it wasn't relevant to his becoming a tax lawyer. He just put up with the course," said Dr. Herring. "I didn't know him very well, but he took the tests and passed the course."

"When John became a writer," Dr. Herring continued, "I asked him to come talk to the accounting students here because writing and communicating are very important skills even in this field."

On one of these visits, Dr. Herring asked John Grisham, "Are you sorry you earned an accounting degree?"

"Oh no," replied Grisham. "I learned logic and it helped in writing and in law. If I had gone through a writer's course, I might not have had my own style. My style and creativity might have been modified."

According to Dr. Herring, there is a great loyalty to Mississippi State University from graduates. "Most of the students...perhaps 85%...come from small towns in Mississippi. In the summer time, the campus is used as a summer camp. Many children have come summer after summer and feel an attachment to the university. Parents come to visit, too. A special feeling develops from childhood days. If the children become students, an even stronger bond is built."

With only two years on campus as a student, John Grisham felt a strong bond. He went back again and again for football and baseball games to see the Bulldogs play in their maroon and white uniforms.

But his biggest bond was with the Dudy Noble Baseball field. Once he graduated in 1977, Grisham would come back regularly to watch those college baseball games. He described his reasons in an introduction to a book about MSU Baseball. "It's great baseball played by very talented kids. The game is pure and uncorrupted by money. The place is filled with memories, both of my college days and of the great games and moments since then. It's a wonderful place to unwind. The food is plentiful. The people are happy. The mood is festive. Time is meaningless. The game is played without a clock. There are no telephones in Left Field. Deadlines are more distant. Appointments seem insignificant."

Grisham's favorite place at an MSU baseball game was to sit on top of an old pickup truck, painted maroon, with friends, enjoying the food and talk. Out on the Left Field Lounge, the trucks and trailers have their own spots. Food and hospitality were the unwritten rules. Unshaven, Grisham felt at home. But with fame had come recognition. This celebrity intruded on his freedom. Often he would arrive in disguise, hiding from the fans and public. Forced into greater seclusion, Grisham and his wife purchased a private skybox, overlooking the field. Here he can have food and friends without interference.

Many years after graduation and before Grisham's fame, John had come back to MSU to watch the team play against Brigham Young University. John's group of friends adopted the visiting team to feed them and make them feel welcome. The opposing team was sick of eating fast food and readily accepted the invitation to eat.

Grisham recalled that incident. "We fed them for three hours. Late in the game, I sat next to one of the BYU players and watched with amusement as he tried to eat crayfish. He'd already been served spareribs, pork shoulder, catfish, frog legs, steak and smoked sausage, and as we watched the game I helped with the crayfish. A dense, charcoal fog hung over left field. The mob pushed toward the fence."

"The kid was awestruck. I've seen this reaction many times from ballplayers, and for some reason I always felt compelled to share my knowledge of Dudy Noble and its legends. I filled his ear. Someone passed up a plate of boiled shrimp, and he quickly forgot about the crayfish. I told him legendary stories about Polk."

Ron Polk is the beloved baseball coach who arrived at MSU after Grisham left. He is as famous to MSU's baseball team as Bear Bryant was to the University of Alabama's Crimson Tide football team. With a round baby-face, Polk affectionately calls everyone "Babe" or "Baby." In recent years Polk and Grisham have given many speeches together for charity. They have a sparring, humorous relationship and entertain their audiences with spicy remarks.

As John Grisham continued to fill this BYU student with the history of Left Field Lounge and Dudy Noble Field as a one-time cow pasture, Grisham wrote, "It was quite a performance, really. He didn't hear a word. He ate his shrimp and watched the chefs at play in the fog. He studied the zany architecture of the trailers and trucks and vans packed together. He stared at the crowd of nine thousand rowdies who had gathered for a college baseball game. 'Unbelievable' said the BYU player. 'I wish I had played here.'"

Ten years after Grisham graduated, he returned once again to one of the baseball games. During this visit, he thought back to the time he sat alone in the bleachers, thinking about his future and the realization that he would not become an all-star baseball player.

Grisham wrote, "As fate would have it, two young college boys sat in front of me. The game was boring, and I found myself listening to their conversation. One of them was a sophomore, and very confused, uncertain of his major, undecided about most everything, even contemplating a transfer to another school. It was me—thirteen years earlier. I didn't say a word. I didn't know him, and I was over thirty, so he wouldn't have listened anyway. But I had so much to tell him, so much wonderful advice. I smiled to myself as he poured his heart out to his friend. I wanted so badly to put my hand on his shoulder and simply say, 'You've come to the right place.'"

Before John Grisham finished his college days at State, he had a short fling at writing fiction. In his senior year, he had a story idea about an international terrorist plot that would take place on a university campus. Today, in the 21st century, that would be a timely plot. He was 30 years ahead of his time in thinking through original storylines. Also he had some ideas for plots about small Mississippi towns and their residents. Little did he realize that those infant ideas might grow up into full-blown novels.

And so, as John Grisham received his B.S. degree in accountancy, he would advance to the next chapter in his life…law school.

5

OLE MISS AND ROMANCE

From the open spaces of Starkville, John Grisham moved north to the enchanted small town of Oxford, Mississippi. Here he would spend three years in law school at the University of Mississippi.

Oxford has a mystical charm that draws Mississippians and outsiders alike. The town population fluctuates around 10,000. The student population equals that of the town. Frequently, Oxford appears on lists as one of the most desirable places to live or retire in the United States. For one thing, it is a college town. With only 600 acres—now expanded to 2,500, the University campus is a cocoon, secluded and surrounded by the town itself. Students often gravitate to Oxford's town square, only two or three miles from the center of the campus for a taste of everyday southern life.

In the heart of the square is a gleaming white courthouse, Lafayette County Courthouse, softened by the magnolia trees around it. Inside, the rotunda is somber and the walls of dark wood. Offices at the top of the stairs are small, and files are stacked under and above the shelves. Lawyers, in their best-tailored suits, linger outside to talk and then walk purposefully inside with their leather shoes echoing in the Chamber.

Around the courthouse on the four sides of the square are two-storied shops and restaurants. They are attached—not unlike New Orleans. Only the streets, merging from the four corners, separate the sides. Wrought iron balconies are above each storefront. The shops are in white or pastel colors with ornate decorated windows and doors. Because of its architectural elegance, the square could be a movie set from pre-Civil War days.

The focal point of the square is the now famous bookstore, Square Books, owned by Richard Howorth. His clients...students, residents, and tourists...browse in the comfortable, high-ceiling store. They are invited to sit down and read *The New York Times*. But mostly, people are browsing for books by William Faulkner, Eudora Welty, Larry Brown, Barry Hannah, and of course, John

Grisham—all Mississippi writers of note. Discounts are of no import to these buyers. Atmosphere is. They feel caught up in the nostalgia of the old South and of William Faulkner's fictional and unpronounceable *Yoknapatawpha County.*

When students want to dress up and impress their girl friends, they take them to the restaurants on the square. When parents come to visit, they are steered to the square also. Rich southern food is the fare. Cajun catfish, soaked in cream sauce, with hot cornbread was and is a favorite of John Grisham's at the Downtown Grill with its rosewood tables, green walls, and prints of hunting scenes. Unshaven, he usually would sit upstairs in less elegant surroundings, after a book signing, and watch people on the square. Crayfish salad with red pepper roulade dressing and cornbread is a lighter part of the menu.

Familiar fast food restaurants hover on the flanks of the square to feed students on limited allowances. The bakeries, indulging in rich pastries and large cups of hot coffee, do a booming business on Sunday mornings before and after church services.

On the fringes of the square is a cluster of Protestant churches within blocks of each other. Some are red brick and some are yellow brick. Some have soaring white steeples and some don't. But they all have majestic arched entrances. For most towns throughout the south, the church is the heart and soul of life for families and single people. Sunday services and Wednesday night prayer meetings are the major days of the week. Church brunches, suppers, and sports activities can fill every weekend. Choir practice and Sunday School keep young people occupied.

When John Grisham arrived in Oxford, he attended the First Baptist Church in Oxford. The church had a long history, dating back to 1842. On Sunday mornings, Sunday School for college students was a discussion group for an hour. Afterwards, the young people streamed into the main edifice, carrying their Bibles in one hand and sitting on the side pews.

Music was the main part of the service. Some members played the piano, organ, or saxophone. Others performed in a small combo or sang in a choir. Sometimes there would be a solo singer. The sermon was short, usually ten or fifteen minutes. No one stayed bored.

The town of Oxford has a rather interesting history. Chickasaw Indians lived in Lafayette County in the early 1800s and even earlier. By 1935 three businessmen set up a country store on the empty land now known as The Square. T.D. Isom, nephew to one of the men, had a dream for his uncle's town. He wanted it to be named "Oxford" after Oxford University in England. Isom hoped the

American town would have its own university. His wish was fulfilled in 1848 when the University of Mississippi opened its doors to 80 students.

Only the Civil War in the 1860s interrupted classes. Some of the students offered to fight against the northern soldiers, but they were killed at Gettysburg, Pennsylvania, in 1863. The Union troops occupied the campus in 1862 under the command of General Ulysses S. Grant. The administration building, called the Lyceum, was used as a hospital for the wounded men of the Union Army.

Against the throbbing history of Indians and the Civil War, surrounding a small, remote university, John Grisham enrolled as a new law student in the fall of 1978.

Everyone referred to the University of Mississippi as "Ole Miss." In the days of slavery, the lady of the manor or plantation was called respectfully the "ole Miss" by the slaves. A young girl was called the "young miss." In 1897 the Greek Society was putting together the yearbook. A student by the name of Alma Meek suggested that the yearbook be called "Ole Miss." Within two years, the affectionate term was the standard description of the University of Mississippi. Ole Miss was 130 years old when Grisham began his studies there.

Ole Miss is half the size of Mississippi State University. It is shaped like a lady's hoop skirt. The ante-bellum Lyceum Hall is at the waist. Its stately columns reflect the Ionic Greek Revival flavor. The trees, sloping down the two-acre apron, are giant pin and live oaks, shiny magnolias, elms, and rosebuds. Their leafy heads shade the students from the beastly heat in spring, summer, and fall. From the Lyceum, the other buildings spiral down in concentric circles.

One of the most beloved places at Ole Miss is The Grove. At one time it was a nine-acre pasture. Then it became the campus green that abuts The Circle apron. Today, the Grove is full of live and pin oaks, poplars, elms, dogwoods, and rosebuds. The rosebud trees bloom into brilliant purple flowers in spring and the large leaves turn a bright red in fall.

At every home football game, the Grove is full of tailgate parties on Saturday before the game. Year after year, alumni and friends come to the same spot to set up their grills, tables, and buffet spreads. Every inch is taken on The Circle and Grove. The smell of barbecued pork, chicken, and ribs drifts into the nostrils of students and visitors. Some rich people from the Delta land in the northwest part of the state come with their servants. Their tables are set with table clothes and silver while their servants wait on the guests and hosts. Most people at other tables and tents stand, holding their paper plates while they eat. They offer hospitality to any stranger that comes by.

Once the picnics are over, the band marches around the Grove. Then, the Rebel football fans walk to the Vaught-Hemingway stadium for the game. The roars of joy and disappointment echo across the campus and over the whole town of Oxford. At midnight on Saturday, twenty grounds-men sweep through the Grove and the Circle to clean up the mess left during the day. By Sunday morning, the signs of big parties and trash are gone. Only the peaceful grass and trees remain.

Although John Grisham would be introduced to these nostalgic tailgate parties at Ole Miss, they would be familiar to him. He had enjoyed the Left Field Lounge during baseball season at Mississippi State University.

Students also have felt a sentimental attachment to the Grove. Joggers run there or students sit on the grass or benches to study. Often, couples would sit together for hours. Many young men would propose to their sweethearts in the Grove on a balmy spring night and present engagement rings. It was something for married couples to remember in future years, but this tradition has faded with modern times.

According to historian Dr. David Sansing of Ole Miss, William Faulkner's father was on the University staff as business manager. Although his son had not graduated from high school, the university made an exception and let him take classes. The young Faulkner, who was born in Ripley, but eventually lived in Oxford, made a "B" in English and an "A" in Spanish. In future he would become a Nobel Prize winner as a famous southern and American writer.

How ironic that two famous Mississippi writers, Faulkner and Grisham, had ties to Ole Miss: Faulkner in literary fiction and Grisham in commercial fiction. To find out why Mississippi produces such famous writers and musicians has baffled critics for decades.

Historian Dr. Sansing offers some answers. "We are the poorest state in the country and the most backward. We have the highest rate of illiteracy. Yet, we have more Pulitzer Prize winners than any other state," he mused. "Of course, Faulkner was an immense influence. It has been said that Mississippi provides the climate for genius. But we are great storytellers. From the time of the Civil War, uncles and fathers and grandfathers have told and retold the stories of what the Union soldiers did. Even today, someone will remember that his uncle told how Sherman burned his barn. Monuments and cemeteries tell the stories, too." Sansing reflected further on the mysteries of successful writers in Mississippi. He said, "There are strange contradictions to the Mississippi character. We are called the Hospitality State and yet we can express great hostility to outsiders. We have sweet smelling magnolias and the smell of burning crosses from the racially bigoted Ku Klux Klan that burned crosses in the yards of those who were sympathetic or favorable to African/Americans. We can be a very tender and most loving people. But we can also create great acts of cruelty. We are a people of opposites."

"Perhaps small towns offer ideas to our writers," he continued, "because there are no secrets in a small town. Everybody knows everybody and their business. New England and the south have deep roots. The migration of peoples went to the west and Midwest."

Many famous singers come from Mississippi, too. Country singers like Charlie Price and Charlie Pride, Faith Hill, and LeAnn Rimes; opera singer, Leontyne Price; and rock n' roll king, Elvis Presley. Many of these musical gifts start with churches for blacks and whites in the south. Gospel singing inspired the blues and country music. Their songs are usually sad stories about men and women in love or about the struggles of life. Long days of working in the fields and long nights on the plantations wrenched songs from the souls of black slaves and their families.

Against this background of deep emotions, rising from the black earth of the Delta land and the rich red clay of Mississippi, writers like William Faulkner, Willie Morris, and John Grisham have spun their words and stories for the world. One of those writers came to Oxford as a young man, who entered law school with no intention of becoming a writer. He was there to learn the skills of a tax lawyer, hoping to make money from defending rich clients. The young man was John Grisham, Jr. Destiny had something else in mind for him, but lawyering would be part of the process.

His classes would take place mainly in Lamar Hall, only steps from the Grove. The law center is sleek and modern, not southern in architecture. The many-sided sandstone structure sits like a sturdy, functional, chunky block. Inside is a large open common area, covered by large black and white squares of linoleum. Wooden benches are scattered here and there. Most of the classrooms are off the common area. The desks are one long slab of green formica with swinging green plastic chairs, spaced behind them. The desks are tiered and seat about 100 students. The professor stands or sits behind his podium and has a long green blackboard.

Upstairs are offices and the handsome Eastland Law Library. Here students pour over volumes of research and law cases, preparing for their classes. When Grisham had moved to Oxford as a family man and writer, he spent time in the library writing much of *The Pelican Brief* while his house was being built.

Those three years in law school at Ole Miss would change Grisham's life. Although he intended to become a tax lawyer, he soon became bored and disinterested. He found criminal law more fascinating and used to sit in on classes to witness mock trials.

One of Grisham's law professors, who taught a course on "Evidence," vaguely remembered the young law student in his class. Professor Thomas K. Mason said in a soft southern drawl, "I don't remember him too well, but I think he sat in the very back, behind a big guy, so he wouldn't be called on."

Law students very seldom answer questions posed by professors and dread to be called upon. Like the law professor in the television series *The Paper Chase,* the professor can make fun of a student and destroy his argument in front of his or her peers. A law professor also can make a shy and sensitive student feel utterly foolish. Students secretly do crossword puzzles, study for another course, or drift into a dreamy state while in class.

For the most part, Grisham left no strong impressions on the faculty. However, Dr. Guthrie Abbott, a one-time President of the Mississippi Bar, said of his former student, "He was a good student and did well in class. I didn't dream he would write an American novel and movie. I would have said you had the wrong person."

Another professor, Robert Khayat, became Chancellor of Ole Miss in the mid-1990s. While Grisham was in law school, Khayat was his professor on a course dealing with tort (a wrongful injury or damage done to a client). During a very long exam, Grisham wrote and wrote. When he came to the last question, he was tired and didn't know the answer to the question. But he wrote and wrote some more. After Grisham came back from the Christmas holidays, he collected his exam paper. At the bottom, Khayat had written, "You obviously don't know the answer, but you have a great gift for fiction."

During remarks at some Ole Miss ceremonies, John Grisham recalled this little incident for the students. He turned to the Chancellor (Robert Khayat) and asked if he remembered writing those comments. He did. Because Grisham considered Khayat a man of integrity, he concluded his speech by saying, "When I grow up, I want to be just like Robert Khayat." Applause and laughter greeted Grisham.

Amid the grind of law studies, Grisham would come face to face with a tragedy of a friend. It happened to one of his best friends from Mississippi State University. In an interview with *Christianity Today,* Grisham said, "I was in law school, and he called me one day and wanted to get together. So we had lunch, and he told me he had terminal cancer. He was only 25. I couldn't believe it."

Grisham was stunned by his friend's news and wanted to know what one does when one realizes that death will be very soon. The friend replied, "It's real simple. You get things right with God, and you spend as much time with those you love as you can. Then you settle up with everybody else. You know, really, you ought to live every day like you have only a few more days to live."

Those final thoughts made a great impression on John Grisham. "I've never forgotten my friend's advice," he said.

But life had lighter moments, too. When young Grisham was home in Southaven from MSU and Ole Miss, he noticed a little girl on the next street. That little girl had turned into a beautiful young teenager. She was Elizabeth Renee Jones. John was six years older than Renee, but he was dazzled by her beauty. She was a tall, slim brunette with startling blue eyes. Grisham said that she was the kid next door who had suddenly grown up. Friends claim that it was love at first sight for both.

One of the Grisham neighbors in Southaven noted that Renee was a topnotch student in English and Literature. Apparently, Grisham was more impressed with the fact that Renee could play basketball and never sweat.

While Renee was a senior in high school and John was a first year law student, the letters passed frequently between Southaven and Oxford. Renee has confessed that his love letters were an indication that John Grisham was a good writer. Then, she came to Ole Miss for two years, majoring in English Literature. They became a steady couple. By the spring of 1980, John Grisham took Renee to a romantic setting in the Grove and proposed, presenting Renee with an engagement ring.

The prospect of supporting a wife in another year gave Grisham reason to intensify his studies.

This is Main Street in Black Oak, Arkansas, where Grisham grew up until the age of six or seven. Even today, the population is 200.

Young John Grisham attended Monette Elementary School in Monette, Arkansas. It was only 3 or 4 miles from Black Oak.

When Grisham's parents moved to Southaven, Mississippi, they lived in this house on Coventry Cove Road, which is close to the high school.

Grisham graduated from Southaven High School in 1973 while living in Southaven, Mississippi.

John Grisham studied accounting in McCool Hall at Mississippi State University, where he earned a BS degree.

This is the Law School at the University of Mississippi in Oxford where Grisham studied for three years.

The Grishams built this yellow Victorian farmhouse on the main highway
outside Oxford, Mississippi. It is highly visible to tour buses and visitors.

The First Baptist Church in Oxford, Mississippi, was the place where John
and Renee were married and became members.

The first house Renee and John Grisham owned as newlyweds was on Farmington Road in Southaven.

Here is Grisham's first law office in Southaven, Mississippi. His office was upstairs on the left.

The De Soto County courthouse in Hernando, Mississippi, where his novel, "A Time to Kill," was set.

The Belfry in Oxford, Mississippi, where Grisham's secretary works. There is a display of all his books inside.

The Mississippi State capital in Jackson, Mississippi, where Grisham was a legislator from 1983 to 1991.

John Grisham

John Grisham in second grade.

The John Grisham Special Collections Room in the Mitchell Library at Mississippi State University at Starkville, Mississippi.

William Faulkner's plantation home,"Rowan Oak," in Oxford, Mississippi.

6

BECOMING A STREET LAWYER

John Grisham graduated from law school in May of 1981. He was the first in his family to graduate from college and certainly the first and only one to graduate from law school. His parents worked hard to send their children to college. It wasn't a matter of choice. The Grisham parents required their children to attend college. In retrospect, Grisham advises young people to stay in school as long as they can—even to the age of thirty.

But there was something far more important than a law degree to John Grisham. It was Renee Jones. His very next step was to marry this southern beauty.

Coming from a big family, Grisham might have had a big wedding with his brothers and sisters as groomsmen and bridesmaids. But John Grisham, true to his character, had a very private wedding. On May 8, 1981, Dr. Lewis Sewell, pastor of the First Baptist Church in Oxford, married this handsome young couple.

John and Renee had obtained their marriage license in Southaven, but Oxford was their choice for the wedding. After all, they had both gone to Ole Miss; the town was filled with memories and charm; it was William Faulkner's home. Oxford was the perfect setting for marriage.

The pastor's study was a favorite place for young couples to say their vows. The study was on the corner of the Sunday School building. Sewell's office had three walls covered with books. The wall behind his dark-stained desk had photos and official degrees framed. His back was to the street in his chair. There was a leather recliner. The young couple only had eyes for each other—not the furnishings of the pastor's office. John and Renee stood in front of the desk while Dr. Sewell read from the Scriptures, and they recited their marriage vows. Only one witness was present.

Dr. Sewell, whose offices have moved to Tupelo, Mississippi, didn't recall marrying the now famous Grishams. "I married so many young couples that I didn't remember John and Renee. Not until I telephoned the offices in Southaven and learned I was the pastor on the certificate, was that fact revealed," he said.

After the honeymoon, the next move for the newlyweds was to find a place to live and for John to become a real lawyer. They returned to their roots—Southaven, Mississippi. They both had grown up there. People in the community and church knew them and both sets of parents lived close to each other.

The young couple found a two-bedroom ranch made of red brick and white wood with a carport to house their cars. It was on Farmington Road next to the Joneses (Renee's parents). John's parents were on the next street on Coventry Cove. John and Renee were back home in their neighborhood where they had spent their teen years. Southaven High School was within walking distance.

Building a law practice was the immediate object of the new husband. John Grisham had to take his law school knowledge and polish his skills as a new, young lawyer. Unlike Mitch McDeere—the leading character in *The Firm*, John Grisham was not hounded and sought after to join big law firms across the country. In a self-interview in *U.S.A. Weekend* in 1993, Grisham speaks to this issue. "Believe it or not, I was not heavily recruited by firms when I finished law school. In fact, no one offered me a job. But, I had a couple of close friends who were top students, and they were wined and dined by big law firms throughout the Southeast. Vicariously, I lived through this search for employment with them. They compared offers from firms. There were basics such as salary, type of work, partnerships, the usual boilerplate inherent in any interview. The fun part was discussing the perks the various firms used to entice…things such as country club memberships, cars, vacation condos."

None of those perks were offered to young John Grisham. Instead, he found a simple office on the corner of Stateline and Airways Road in Southaven. The location was central and a short distance from the De Soto Country Courthouse in Hernando, Mississippi. Barry Bouchillon, an insurance agent, owned the building. One side belonged to Barry's insurance company and the other side was rented to Grisham, who eventually had a partner, Larry Vaughn.

The modern building looked more like two townhouses joined together. The outside was a combination of red brick and a dusty beige wood. Two gables projected from the second story roof. The reception area was on the ground floor. Nestled under the stairs was a small conference room for meeting clients.

Upstairs were two small offices, crowded with desks, files, and papers. The tray ceiling was rather interesting. A rectangular portion of it had a mocha-colored wallpaper that Grisham liked. Plenty of parking was available outside.

When Grisham gave the commencement address in 1992 to graduates of Mississippi State University and reminisced about his dreams and plans for the future, he said, "When I sat out there fifteen years ago, I was rather smug and confident, perhaps even a bit arrogant because I, at the age of twenty-two, had already figured out my life. I had it all planned, and was certain things would fall neatly into place. I had earned my degree in accounting. I had been accepted to law school where I planned to study tax law and one day soon make lots of money representing rich people who didn't want to pay taxes. My goal was to become a successful lawyer, and there was no doubt it would happen. Everything was planned."

"...I returned to my hometown of Southaven, hung out my shingle, and declared myself ready to sue. I worked hard, treated people fairly, and soon was very busy."

The purpose of his talk was to tell those young graduates something about plans for the future. "If you are sitting out there now with a nice, neat little outline for the next ten years, you'd better be careful. Life may have other plans. Life will present you with unexpected opportunities, and it will be up to you to take a chance, to be bold, to have faith, and go for it. Life will also present you with bad luck and hardship, and maybe even tragedy, so get ready for it. It happens to everyone."

Talking to young people is a passion with John Grisham. He repeats this theme of staying in college again and again to students or journalists that interview him. "I love to talk to kids and ask them where they're going to college, and what they want to study. And so often, it's all planned. They know exactly what they're going to do and where they're going to be ten years from now. I don't want to dampen their enthusiasm, but I want to say, 'You can't plan everything.' I didn't plan to write books, it was not something I ever thought about. I thought I'd be a lawyer for the rest of my life. It's important to have goals and to work hard for them, but life has a way of presenting opportunities that you don't really notice at first. Success a lot of times depends on whether you make a change and try something you hadn't planned, something new. I give commencement speeches occasionally to colleges and high schools, and I usually dwell on that, tell the students, Get your education and work hard, but don't race toward the age of 22 or 23 when you're out of college, and you've got the credit card, and you've got the BMW, and you want everything right then at the age of 23, because you're not going to enjoy your education. I tell kids to stay in school until they're 30."

As a new member of the Mississippi bar in 1981, John Grisham began his law practice in his country hometown. For ten years he would specialize in personal-injury, litigation, and criminal defense.

In his own words, Grisham described his feelings about those ten years. "My law career was not very fulfilling. I was a street lawyer, one of a thousand in a profession that was and is terribly overcrowded. Competition was fierce; ethics were often compromised; and I could never bring myself to advertise."

Grisham further explained, "When I was actively practicing law, there were cases and clients I refused to take because of my faith. I didn't do divorce work because the laws are now such that divorce is too easy. I turned down certain criminal defendants because I couldn't bring myself to believe them or fight for them. I did a lot of pro bono work for churches with an assortment of legal problems."

Apparently Grisham's first jury trial was, according to him, a gruesome case. He defended a man who had shot his wife's lover six times in the head. The shooting was done at pointblank range. Grisham argued that his client had acted in self-defense because the lover had aimed and fired a shot at him from a .22 caliber pistol. The bullet glanced off his client's chest. Grisham won the case. A neighbor of Grisham's disputed the circumstances and outcome of the case after it was over. Nothing was said, but Grisham responded with a broad grin.

Grisham told a local newspaper, "About half of my practice was criminal defense and a good chunk was plaintiffs litigation, personal injury suits, workman's compensation, wrongful death suits, and a little domestic stuff, though not much."

When this author interviewed Harry Randolph Garner, a country lawyer in a law office on the county courthouse square in Hernando, Mississippi, and the model for the Rex Vonner character in Grisham's first novel, *A Time to Kill*, Garner said, "When he was a young lawyer, Grisham was star-struck, but he did well. As a trial lawyer, he was at first inept. Law is a philosophy of thinking. When Grisham first got his license, he took a case no one else would. Grisham and his partner mortgaged their home and made a good recovery. Grisham had the Midas touch with everything."

The case to which Garner referred happened in 1982. Grisham described the case this way, "The case involved a little boy who'd been badly burned by a water heater explosion. His father came to my office on a DUI charge. I wasn't real busy, so we talked. One thing led to another. I sued the manufacturer of the heater, claiming the explosion could have been prevented. I settled that suit in 1983—two years out of law school. My portion of the fee was $50,000, and I thought that was all the money in the world."

Grisham and H.R. Garner had one final successful case together in the 1980s. "That last case we had was about two black people in a 1972 Toyota station wagon," recalled Garner. "The vehicle was hit in the rear end and the frame locked the windows. One of the passengers was killed. We represented the younger man. A white man hit the car. Although the car was out of gas, there were gas tanks in the car and they exploded. We settled with Toyota. And yet, in a similar case with the same vehicle in Texas, Toyota won."

When Grisham used Garner for a character in *A Time to Kill*, Garner was a big, heavy-set man, wearing suspenders and sporting a square mustache. Today, Garner is 50 pounds lighter, clean-shaven, and soft-spoken. A model country lawyer, one or two of his clients keep Garner on a retainer basis in case their spouses divorce them. His reputation as a skilled and unbeatable lawyer has spread the length and breadth of Mississippi. No one crosses Harry Garner.

Garner reflected on Grisham's character during an interview and offered this analysis, "His strongest qualities? He is idealistic and has principles. He believes in less government and more for the individual. He's not greedy; he's faithful to his wife; and no drinking. On the other hand, he can be brooding and doesn't forget slights. But he has been generous to churches of different denominations and donated as much as $100,000."

Another observer of Grisham's legal work was Judge Toby Wilson, who was a judge on a workman's compensation case that Grisham tried, remembered the case and Grisham in the mid-1980s.

"Grisham represented a claimant in Hernando and he won," Judge Wilson recalled. "As we were walking to our cars parked on the square, John turned to me and said, 'Judge, I'm going to write the great American novel.' I smiled and replied, 'Here, John, read this book on Workman's Compensation. I think you could make a good living from these cases.' When his first book was published, John sent me an autographed copy that was inscribed, 'I told you so.'"

Hernando, Mississippi, where the De Soto County Courthouse is located, has a picturesque quality, not unlike Oxford, Mississippi. The square around the courthouse is the heart of the town. The red brick courthouse with its six white columns is set back from the street. Sturdy white oak trees and shiny magnolia trees cover and shade the grassy lawn in front. On three sides of the square are shops, cafes, and offices—some double-story ones overlook the square from wrought iron balustrades.

Inside the courthouse, voices of lawyers in their dark suits echo in the rotunda as their leather shoes scuff over the red and white star under the dome above. A wrought iron railing circles the second story. Scenes of Hernando De Soto, the Spanish explorer, greeting native Indians, are painted on the walls. The court-room on the second floor looks more like a small chapel with its oak pews, judge's pulpit, and jury box. Behind the courtroom are holding rooms for prisoners brought up the twin back stairs.

Here, John Grisham tried many cases during his ten years as a practicing lawyer. Here, too, he would set the dramatic trial of his first novel, *A Time to Kill.* Those twin back stairs would play an important, but violent role in that novel. Here he would find rich ideas for many of his novels.

There would be other interests for John Grisham besides lawyering. He and his wife Renee would start a family—a son, Ty, and a daughter, Shea. Grisham would become a solid member of the Rotary Club, often arranging entertainment for the group. He and Renee joined the Baptist Church. They moved from the downtown Baptist Church to the Carriage Hills Baptist Church at the other end of Farmington Road. It was nearer to their home. Renee and John would teach Sunday School there. John taught 7th and 8th graders and would sometimes take his class bowling on a Saturday.

The minister of the Carriage Hills Baptist Church, Reverend David Merritt, knew John's parents and Renee's parents from his congregation. Every year when David Merritt and his wife wanted to take a vacation, Big John Grisham would come by their house and give them the keys to his Chevrolet van to use on their vacation. Young John and Renee would come to Wednesday night prayer meetings and to the church suppers.

"Renee was very attractive, sweet, and had high standards. John was a high caliber person, conservative, and a gentleman. He was somewhat introverted and didn't speak until he was spoken to, "said Reverend Merritt in an interview. "I remember our Rotary meetings. Afterwards we often went up to John's office, put our feet up on the conference table, and swapped stories."

Reverend Merritt commented on the closeness of the Grisham family. "If a death occurred in the family, the Grishams would think nothing of driving 200 miles to attend the funeral of a relative as a family group. Young John was very generous to the church when he became famous. Without any publicity, he bought a coach bus for $55,000 to be used to help people in need in the event of tornadoes, floods, or other natural tragedies. Women from the church would drive to these areas and provide meals and necessities."

During the early 1980s, John Grisham became restless. He was persuaded in 1983 to run for the Mississippi legislature, which meets for six weeks of every year in the state capital of Jackson, about 200 miles south of Southaven. Grisham was elected to a four-year term, representing the Seventh District in the local House of Representatives.

In a newspaper interview Grisham was quoted, "I beat a 20-year incumbent. That was a lot of fun, like winning a big ball game." He went to serve his state, hoping that maybe he could make some changes, especially in the field of public education. Grisham believed that he could still run his law office and serve effectively as a state government representative. He would leave on a Tuesday morning to drive from Southaven to Jackson. He returned home on a Thursday. The two nights in Jackson were spent on a spare bed with old friends like Bobby Moak or Scott Ross.

The state capitol is located in an awesome location. Right in the heart of Jackson, the 1903 state house might be mistaken for the state capitol in Washington, D.C., except for the square grounds, Japanese magnolias, and oak trees surrounding the building. At night the illuminated dome is breathtaking. On top is a copper eagle, painted in gold leaf and with a wingspan of 15 feet. On either side of the front entrance and its steep staircase sits a reproduction of the cracked Liberty Bell and an impressive bronze statue of confederate women. It is a memorial for their devotion to the confederate soldiers during the Civil War.

Only tourists or visitors climb the stairs to the front entrance. The 52 senators and 122 members of the House of Representatives park and go through the back entrance as do most others. A certain hush comes over those who enter the impressive edifice. Echoes from voices and the clip clop of shoes bounce off the white marble walls, bordered by black marble, and soar up the three stories under the spiral-wheeled rotunda made from exotic marble. The ground floor is decorated with marble columns. Wrought iron railings circle the second and third floors of the rotunda.

The two chambers are decorated with Belgian black marble and all the chairs are leather. They are large and comfortable and swivel. In the senate chamber is a dome of Bohemian stained glass. As a new member in the 1984 session, Grisham sat near the back.

Because Grisham was newly elected and not chairman of a committee, he did not qualify for an inside office. Instead he had a small cubicle on the mezzanine with a desk, but he was in and out of other people's offices using their desks and telephones.

According to Peggy Martin, executive secretary to the Judiciary Committee, the young female pages loved the handsome Grisham and called him "cute." Martin said in an interview, "John was dedicated to home, church, and family. He always talked about his wife and how much he loved her and claimed she was the best looking woman in the world. He was very friendly, humorous, and clever. Many of the members thought he wrote the newsletters. It was supposed to be anonymous. Frankly, John found it too frustrating being in the legislature. Trying to get things done and bills passed took too long. There would be 1,800 bills introduced a year and only a few would pass. Besides the salary was only $10,000 a year. A per diem was paid only for the days spent at the state capitol. Grisham spent two or three days a week in Jackson."

However, Grisham made some good and lasting friends during his political career of seven years. Edwin Perry, a lawyer from Oxford, Mississippi, became a close family friend. At the time Grisham was a legislator, Perry was Vice-Chairman of the Appropriations Committee. Grisham ran Perry's campaign to become Speaker of the House. A skilled politician, Perry could see that Grisham was impatient with the tedium and lengthy process of the legislature. Ed Perry would play a key role in launching Grisham's writing career.

Meanwhile, Grisham was Vice-Chairman of Committee on Apportionment and Elections, and he was a member of State Democratic Executive Committee from 1988 to 1990. All of this political experience would become another resource once he became a writer.

One simple incident in Hernando, Mississippi, would slowly turn Grisham's life in a completely new direction…something unexpected.

7

THE FIRST NOVEL

When Grisham wasn't wandering the halls and chambers at the state capitol January, February, and part of March, he was busy at the courthouse in Hernando on Mondays and Fridays, keeping his law practice afloat. A continued sense of restlessness and dissatisfaction with the law and politics gave him a feeling of being unsettled and unhappy.

That feeling began to change one day early in 1984 when Grisham was at the De Soto County courthouse and not very busy. He decided to slip into the little courtroom on the second floor and listen to whatever case might be on trial. Sitting on the back row reserved for the public, Grisham heard something so powerful that his mind and heart were jolted and forever changed.

In an interview with *People* magazine Grisham described his experience, "This ten-year-old girl was testifying against a man who had raped her and left her for dead. I never felt such emotion and human drama in my life. I became obsessed wondering what it would be like if the girl's father killed the rapist and was put on trial. I had to write it down."

The gripping words of the girl riveted every eye on her. Apparently, she related the rape events in a matter of fact way. But the courtroom was silent and electrified. Tears rolled uncontrollably down the cheeks of the listeners. John Grisham's throat was tight and he had to choke back the tears. When it was over, he was drained.

Grisham couldn't get this scene out of his mind. He saw and heard the girl testifying over and over in his thoughts. During the drive back and forth to Jackson, he could think of nothing else. An outline started to evolve. By November 20, 1984 Grisham flipped the cover of an empty stenographer's spiral notebook and began to write in longhand.

Somehow Grisham was driven to write. He couldn't stop. Every morning he went to his office in Southaven at 5:00 a.m. and wrote for three hours. Then he turned to his law practice. He was working about 80 hours a week.

In an interview with a journalism instructor at the University of Mississippi, he said, "With the first two books, I got up at five in the morning. I'd tell myself I had to be at my desk with my first cup of coffee by 5:30. Those little games you play with yourself work. I told myself that in the first 30 minutes, I had to get my first page out of the way."

"I wrote with the flu, on vacation, with no sleep, in courthouses when I could sneak off to a quiet room for 30 minutes in the state capitol building in Jackson. I carried a legal pad with me in my briefcase and wrote on it."

"I'd get sick of it. I'd want to sleep later some mornings or go to bed early some nights. I had a lot of self-doubt. I'd walk in a bookstore and see all those books and think, "Who wants to read this story I'm writing?' I'd see all those books and think, 'There's no room for me up there.' I'd see articles about how Americans don't read much anymore. There are always thousands of reasons not to do something. You can always think of more reasons not to do it than to do it."

"But I never abandoned the book. I was always thinking about it. Still, if my wife, Renee, hadn't been full of encouragement, I wouldn't have finished it. It also helped to read *Writer's Digest*."

After Grisham finished the first chapter of his first novel, he let his wife read it. She liked it and wanted to read more. Finding the right title took more time. At first, he called it *Deathknell*. When he finished the novel, Grisham turned to the book of Ecclesiastes in the Bible and found "A Time for Everything." He considered that phrase as a possible title until, finally, the title of *A Time to Kill* seemed to fit.

When Grisham thinks of those green steno pads filled with the first draft of *A Time to Kill,* he has said, "The original handwritten manuscript…is still impossible for me to look at without a twinge of emotion…I scribbled on these pads at the dining room table, long after Renee and the children were asleep. Many times I cursed the sight of these green pages, but for reasons I cannot fully articulate, I was always drawn back to them."

In 1987—three years from the time he started the book—John Grisham wrote the final words to *A Time to Kill*. It was a fictional story based on the testimony he had witnessed in the courtroom. Basically, the story is about a black Vietnam veteran who murders two young white men because they raped his 12-year-old daughter and dragged her behind their yellow truck. A young white lawyer, Jack Brigance (a Grisham-like character), defends the father. The lawyer has to battle the demonstrations of the vicious and bigoted Ku Klux Klan, who make threats against his own life and his family's, and an all white jury. Grisham set the novel in a mythical Ford County in a small town called Clanton. In reality he used Hernando and the layout of the De Soto County Courthouse for the double murders on the twin backstairs of the courthouse. The opening is a gut-grabber and the reader's interest never lets up.

Once the book was finished, Grisham had some hard questions to answer. What should he do next? How could he sell it? Firstly, he had to have it typed and then Grisham had to research the book industry thoroughly in order to put his plan of attack into action by November of 1987.

In an interview he said, "I sat down with my secretary and we made up two lists. One contained the names and addresses of 30 publishing house editors; the other, 30 names and addresses of literary agents. Having already put together a package containing a query letter, book summary, and the first three chapters, I had the secretary make ten copies of each. She was to send a copy of each to the first five editors on the first list and the same to the first five agents on the second."

"When a rejection came back with the material we had sent, she simply crossed that name off the list and immediately sent the package with a new query letter to the next one on the list. This way, we always had some going out as others were coming back. The rejection letters were filed and I would read them when I went to the office each weekend."

Like any fledgling author, the rejections did come—dozens of them. "I never thought of quitting," he said. "My attitude was: 'What the heck, let's have some fun.' Honestly, I believe I would've sent it to several hundred people before I would have even thought of giving up."

At this point, Grisham turned to his good friend Ed Perry for some help. Perry was based in Oxford as a lawyer. Grisham told his friend that he had written a manuscript for a book and wondered if famous author Willie Morris (a fellow Mississippian and youngest editor of *Harper's* magazine) might help. Perry contacted Morris and the three of them dined together.

Willie Morris described the episode this way, "My friend Ed Perry, the state representative from Oxford, was running for the Speaker-ship of the House and asked me if I'd give some professional advice to the representative from Southaven, who was one of Ed's most active supporters. This was 1988 and the fellow from Southaven was beginning to write a book. His name was Grisham and he apparently wanted to know about literary agents."

"Ed and I met him for dinner at a restaurant in Oxford called J.P.'s, one of our hangouts at the time. I liked John and could tell he was serious about wanting to write. He told me he had recently compiled a list from trade journals of dozens of literary agents around the country and sent letters and samples of his writing to these people. Most had not given him the courtesy of a reply. The replies he did get were negative with one exception, an agent in New York named Garon."

"I had not had dealings with the man during my publishing days in New York. I promised John to check him out. I also advised him on such matters as an agent's commission, and to beware especially of any agent who asked for front money, and that there were legitimate agents and fly-by-night agents," according to Morris.

"I telephoned an old friend in New York, Bob Loomis, the head man at Random House, one of the country's finest editors, and told him of Grisham's situation. He phoned back in a couple of days and said Garon was indeed 'legit.' "

Grisham signed a contract with Jay Garon as his agent. When Garon was interviewed for the *Agent and Manager* publication in 1991, he was asked about his new client. "I love discovering new writers. It's an excitement for me to develop a new writer...it's such a satisfaction. He sent me a very interesting query letter after approaching 16 agents...and I was the only one that responded. He sent the manuscript when I asked for it."

After Garon spent a year trying to sell the manuscript through 17 submissions, Wynwood Press, a small New York publisher, decided to publish it and gave Grisham $15,000 as an advance. Like most books, the editing and actual publishing took another year. In 1989 they printed 5,000 copies in hardback covers. Wynwood had been a religious publishing house, printing the magazine *Guideposts,* and slowly moved into secular books. Bill Thompson was the editor-in-chief. Ironically, Wynwood Press and Bill Thompson had discovered another writer, Stephen King, and acquired a number of his novels.

According to Jay Garon, "The company more or less let us down...they didn't do any advertising and promotion. We had very, very good reviews, but it wasn't selling because nobody knew the existence of this author, and most of the reviews were in the areas where the company shipped to."

Like many authors, John Grisham purchased 1,000 copies of his book and tried desperately to sell them all around the state of Mississippi. The retail price was $18.95 per copy and Grisham was able to purchase them for $10 each. From the back of his Volvo station wagon, Grisham drove to autograph signing parties and teas at libraries, garden clubs, and bookstores in his state.

One of his first signings was at the M.R. Davis Library in Southaven. Convinced he would sign all 1,000 copies there, Grisham was greatly disappointed when only 187 were sold. There was another public offering in Jackson where he invited his political colleagues for the book signing. Most of his friends joked about the book and teased him, saying that Renee really wrote it. But Ed Perry recognized the talent of his friend and bought 75 copies. Willie Morris had written a statement about the book, which appeared on the book's jacket, giving it even more prestige.

Richard Howorth, owner of Square books in Oxford, relates with dry humor how John Grisham approached him the first time about a book signing for *A Time to Kill.* "John came in to see me just after he signed with an agent. He told me he wanted to have his first signing at Square Books and wanted to sell 500 copies. I told him we needed to talk. "The grim reality is, John, we cannot sell 500. Our staff has to be enthusiastic about the books we sell and none of us has read your book." At that moment, he thumped a box on the table. There was the typed copy. With a feeling of burden and regret I took the book home. I was up until 2:00 a.m. reading it. It was a great book. I knew we would sell a lot. So, I sent out almost 500 postcards. I paid for the postage and John paid for the printing. We only sold 50 at the signing, but over the next year we sold 500. However, I thought it was better than the book that won the national book award that year."

Sometimes in his novels, Grisham tucks in something personal that the general reading public wouldn't even discover. For example, there are two small personal items in *A Time to Kill.* The first is the mention of Mrs. Pickle's cat. Parker Pickle, if you remember, was John's roommate at several colleges. His mother was a favorite of John's. The second item was the first name of the woman on the jury in *A Time to Kill.* The woman's name was Wanda (the name of Grisham's mother). Wanda turned the jury around to acquit the black father who murdered his daughter's rapists. In later novels, he refrained from planting those personal items.

On the promotion of his first novel, Grisham recounted an autographing experience he had. "Shortly after *A Time to Kill* was published in 1989, I was on the campus of Mississippi State trying desperately to unload a few of the books...I had purchased 1,000 copies, and had already learned the painful lesson that selling books was more difficult than writing them. There was a rather small crowd munching cookies and sipping punch in the library, and it seemed to me as if most of these good folks were being polite yet trying to hang onto their money. This was not the first library I had wedged myself into, and I had become adept at reading the crowds." Today, those first editions in hardback are worth almost $5,000 each. The reason they are so valuable is that there were only 5,000 printed. Since then, millions of paperbacks have been printed.

Although Grisham did not sell many books at his own university, something else positive happened. "The librarian approached me and asked if anyone had asked to collect my papers. I had no idea what he was talking about.

He explained that the library would like to set up a small corner in which to gather and compile my literary, legislative, and legal papers.

Every lawyer dreams of finding someone willing to take his old papers and files, so I readily agreed. I immediately returned home, cleaned out my office, and sent down several boxes of materials, which, until then, had been destined for the landfill. Suddenly, it seemed, they had value. Other boxes have since followed, and the small corner has yielded to a larger room."

In fact, in 1998, a $13 million John Grisham Room and Special Collections Library were established on the top floor of the new Mitchell Memorial Library at Mississippi State University.

All this attention did not mean that John Grisham was rich overnight. The money made from *A Time to Kill* was not enough for Grisham to give up his law practice. He had to keep working and pounding the halls of the county courthouse and the corridors of the state house in Jackson. His family needed that financial support.

With only one book published, Grisham was still an unknown author. He could point to that book on his desk and be proud of its publication, but he wasn't satisfied. He wanted to do more as an author and achieve some kind of recognition.

The future would bring new projects and a new lifestyle that he never could have dreamed about or even imagined.

8

A BEST-SELLING AUTHOR

While Grisham was waiting for his agent to sell his first novel, he couldn't contain his curiosity and called Garon every few days to find out if anything had happened. This irritated Garon. Because it took a year to sell the book, Garon didn't want to be bugged for a whole year by his new client. Instead, he told the author to start writing a second book. Since Grisham was in the routine and rhythm of writing every day, he accepted his agent's advice.

Very quickly Grisham put together a short outline and sent it to Jay Garon, who thought it sounded exciting and told him to write the complete manuscript. From the summer of 1987 until Labor Day of 1989, Grisham worked on *The Firm*. He wrote it in the laundry room of his two-bedroom house. When the washing machine rocked the clothes in its drum, the noise comforted the writer and shut out the world. Although Grisham used legal pads and steno notebooks, he began writing on a PC, using a word processor to hammer out his words and chapters.

Again, Grisham drew upon personal knowledge from his law school years and from observing his fellow law students. The leading character, Mitchell McDeere, wasn't based on Grisham himself, but on a composite of young, aspiring lawyers.

In an interview with a reporter from *Writer's Digest,* Grisham described his life as an author. "…writing is lonely. Nobody can help you. I remember being so tired during the writing of the first two books. An outline is crucial. It saves so much time. When you write suspense, you have to know where you're going because you have to drop little hints along the way. With the outline I always know where the story is going. So before I ever write, I prepare an outline of 40 or 50 pages."

"First, I need a good story idea. Then I sit down and flesh it out. I do an outline to see if the story will work. I show it to my wife, Renee, and to my agent and my editor. On the rare occasions when all four of us agree that an outline will work as a book, then I'll go write the book."

Grisham told the reporter how he keeps the suspense going in his books, "You have to start with an opening so gripping that the reader becomes involved. In the middle of the book, you must sustain the narrative tension and keep things stirred up. The end should be so compelling that people will stay up all night to finish the book. You must have those three elements: how it starts, the end, and what happens in the middle."

"You take a sympathetic hero or heroine, an ordinary person, and tie them into a horrible situation or conspiracy where their lives are at stake. You must keep a lot of sympathy for the heroine or hero. You've got to put them in a situation where they could be killed. That is basic suspense."

"You need a definite plot, conflict and a fast pace. I start with point A and go to B and C and D, and when I get to Z, I'd better be finished or I'm in trouble. The plan is nothing fancy. No flashbacks, no long narratives about relationships. When you're writing suspense, you can't spend a lot of time on persons, places, and settings."

The reporter asked Grisham if he did much research for his books. "I hate to research. I learned to hate it in law school, and I practiced hating it for ten years as a lawyer. Sometimes I'll pay a law student to do legal research. But I'd rather fictionalize a story than do the research."

"For example, *The Firm* is set in Memphis. I grew up in a suburb near Memphis, so I knew the city. I didn't have the time to make a special trip to research a location."

Memphis, Tennessee, would become the setting for Grisham's books, *The Firm* and *The Rainmaker*. Since Southaven, Mississippi, was 30 minutes from downtown Memphis, Grisham knew it well. Usually successful authors write best about the places and people they know. William Faulkner did and Grisham was on his way to doing it.

On the banks of the Mississippi River (3,860 miles long), Memphis was named for the same city in Egypt. The name literally means "established and beautiful." Egypt's Memphis was sited along the Nile River and was filled with pyramids and temples. Tennessee's Memphis has a glass pyramid, constructed along the banks of the river and near to the bridge going to Arkansas. In the 1840s cotton was the staple crop, shipped up and down the river on steamboats and barges. Cotton was called "white gold."

Although the city looks residential and more like a big college town, Memphis has a population of 600,000. The racial mix is half white and half black. Another million people live in the five surrounding counties. The Naval base was the biggest employer during World War II until Fed Ex was founded by Fred Smith in 1972.

Celebrities draw a large tourist population to Memphis. Elvis Presley moved from Mississippi to Memphis when he was 13-years-old. At age 19 in 1954, Presley became a pop star, famous for his singing style and rotating hips while strumming his guitar. When Elvis bought Graceland for his mother, the fans flocked to see it. Even after his death, people of all ages make pilgrimages to Graceland to honor Elvis and his memory.

Other famous names from Tennessee include Supreme Court Justice, Abe Fortas; actress, Cybil Shepherd; and the motel, where Martin Luther King was assassinated on April 4, 1968. During his youth, John Grisham and his friends were fascinated by the action in the city of Memphis. They were drawn to the banks of the city and the bustling nightlife. It was so different from the lazy streets and fields of Southaven. Looking for something to do, young John and his friends often drove to Memphis on the weekends for good food and good music. In those days, Grisham didn't realize that Memphis would become a resource for his novels.

A Memphis law firm plays the leading role in *The Firm*. They are looking for bright young men who come from poor backgrounds. Harvard Law School graduate Mitch McDeere is a poor boy with a bright mind. The biggest and best law firms in the country start wooing him. To entice Mitch, a Memphis law firm dangled some big goodies: a BMW car, a house with a low-interest mortgage, a country club membership, the possibility of becoming a partner, and a starting salary of $80,000. McDeere took the bait. Unknown to him, the firm had some Mafia ties and shady dealings, which McDeere stumbled upon while working as their tax lawyer. At first, he has no idea that his house and car are electronically bugged. The twists and turns and the hero's near misses from death keep the reader up at night, turning page after page.

For the reader, however, the ending of *The Firm* seems somewhat fractured...as if the author were tired of writing the book and couldn't settle on an unexpected outcome. Furthermore, the message of the book appears conflicted. The hero is seduced by money at the beginning. Although Mitch McDeere is driven by ethics and survival to uncover the tax fraud by the Mafia, he is again seduced by money for his own survival in the end. Once he squeals to the FBI about the Mafia, Mitch negotiates a million dollar deal and a place to spend the rest of his days...in the Cayman Islands (one of Grisham's favorite places). Exchanging Mitch's talent for a life of leisure and money does not seem very

Grisham-like although it may be in keeping with the Mitch McDeere character, but not in keeping with Tom Cruise, who has a squeaky clean image. Perhaps, he was miscast.

In a number of Grisham's novels, he ends the book by having his leading character run away to a remote island to live for the rest of his life. When asked if running away was Grisham's secret desire, he replied, "I wanted to run away from the law, but not like my main character. I have a wonderful wife, great kids, a great family. My desire was to make a quick fortune (a typical lawyer's dream) and run away from the profession. Now, though, I'm very content. I can hide from the fame and the public can't find me."

Writing *The Firm* was different from writing *A Time to Kill*. Grisham told a reporter, "I was determined to write clearly, without all the crap. When you write suspense, you want it lean, fast. There's a conscious effort to keep people up all night. I write to grab readers. This isn't serious literature."

After Labor Day of 1989, Grisham sent book number two to his agent Jay Garon. After reading it, Garon said in an interview, "I felt satisfied that I really had a very interesting, exciting, well-written book. I decided to hold an auction. I sent out copies to 14 publishers...and I didn't get too much attention except from Dell and David Gernert at Doubleday."

"The publishing industry is very reticent about paying big money for unknown authors, but the lack of interest from other publishing houses surprised me, because I thought it was one of the best novels I've ever handled...and I've handled some pretty darn good ones."

"Nobody bid against the floor price established by the two representatives, so Doubleday Dell got *The Firm*. While negotiations for *The Firm* were going on in New York, there was action on the West Coast as well...I had sent a xerox copy of the manuscript to my agent, Marti Blumenthal. She did a bang-up job there, and had the movie companies bidding against each other to get this property. Paramount got it."

While publishers and movie agents were scrambling to pick up the rights to *The Firm*, what were John and Renee Grisham doing?

Early on a Sunday morning in 1990, Renee was late dressing for church. She told a reporter, "John had gone ahead to church because he had to stop to buy apple juice for the children he teaches. And I just ran in and said, 'John, you have to go home now and call New York. Some people in Hollywood want to buy *The Firm*. On that Sunday morning, Grisham called Garon and learned the movie rights to his book had been sold for $600,000. Grisham said, "I asked my agent how he got that kind of money for it, and he just said, 'I'm a helluva agent.' And I just said, 'Amen, amen.'"

When asked how he felt upon receiving that amazing phone call, Grisham said, "There have been some wonderful phone calls from New York. The biggest phone call yet was the first time, a truly magical moment. After a year of being turned down, my agent called one day in April of '88 and said, 'We have a publisher for *A Time to Kill*. It's going to be a book.' At that point it had been turned down by 30-something publishers. Everybody had said no to it. He found a very small press in New York, and they wanted to buy it. That was a huge moment.. Another time he called and said, 'We've sold the film rights to *The Firm* to Paramount.' It was totally unexpected, because at that time there was no book deal, it was just in manuscript form. Those are big moments. I don't know if you sort of get jaded, or callous to success, but it's terribly exciting. It's still hard to believe…Something happens every day that makes me stop and try to remember where I am and what's happening."

Shortly after the movie deal, 18 publishers were involved in a bidding frenzy for the book rights. Doubleday won the bidding war with a price of $200,000. Doubleday also signed Grisham to a three-year contract.

The Firm was published in March 1991. Suddenly John and Renee Grisham and their two small children had a sizable amount of money, which would enable them to make some changes in their lives. For a long time, Renee had wanted to go back to Ole Miss to get her degree in English literature. When she married John, she had only completed two years. With only two more years to go to finish her degree, John supported her in this idea. They decided to move to Oxford, Mississippi, a place they both loved. As soon as they moved, Grisham gave up practicing law, and he had resigned his post of seven years as state representative in September 1990. Now he would write full time while Renee finished her university studies.

The Grishams bought almost 70 acres outside the center of Oxford and a mile from the campus on the highway coming into the town. There, they built a yellow Victorian farmhouse on the top of a hill, visible to all who pass by. The young family would live there with two dogs, a cat, and a bird.

An interior decorator, Tim Hargrove, from Birmingham, Alabama, bought antiques for their new home. Hargrove became a friend and when he died, Renee and John drove to Birmingham for the funeral. John even dedicated his book, *The Runaway Jury*, in memory of him.

For his son Ty, Grisham built a baseball diamond on his property. John Grisham would fulfill a lifelong dream by coaching Little League baseball. Wearing his baseball cap backwards and blowing bubble gum, Grisham would shout, praise, and encourage his young team. He loved buying the uniforms and organizing the teams.

As parents, Renee and John took an active part in PTA. One teacher remembers John Grisham coming to Oxford Elementary School to make ice cream sundaes for the class. Others remember how they gave money for a playground at the Bramlet School where Shea attended. They also became active in the First Baptist Church of Oxford where they were married, teaching Sunday School and attending services and social functions.

When *The Firm* went into film production, the Grisham family drove several times to Memphis to watch its filming and visit producer Sydney Pollack and Tom Cruise, who starred as Mitch McDeere.

In *U.S.A. Weekend* of July 1993, Grisham gave a written interview with himself. Humor and modesty emerged from his questions and answers. Asking himself where he would like to see the premier of the movie *The Firm,* he said, "Ideally, I'd like to see it in my den on video with just my wife and a large bowl of microwave popcorn, cheese-flavored."

Grisham's reason for selling the movie rights of his books was, in the beginning, purely for money. He let Hollywood do what they wanted without any interference from him. After six of his books had been made into films, Grisham decided not to sell all of his books to Hollywood. In answer to his earlier hands off attitude to the film world, Grisham replied in his 1993 self-interview, "...I'm full of wisdom right now. Ask me the same question a year from now after all three movies have been released. I may have a different attitude to Hollywood."

Indeed, John Grisham did change his mind about how Hollywood treated his future books. In 2004, Grisham would confess that the filmed version of *The Rainmaker* by Francis Ford Coppola was his favorite movie because it was true to the story, but he wasn't as complimentary about Oliver Stone's interpretation of *The Gingerbread Man.*

As far as selling books, Grisham dreaded the 22-city book tour and media appearances outlined by his publisher. He chose his own book signings, which consisted of five independent bookstores that held autograph parties for him before he was famous. They were: The Square Books in Oxford; Burke's in Memphis; That Bookstore in Blytheville, Arkansas; Lemuria Bookstore in Jackson; and Reeds Gumtree Bookstore in Tupelo, Mississippi. They were loyal to Grisham, and Grisham remained loyal to them by flying there in his own personal airplane. Usually he wore Docker pants, a plaid or denim shirt, and sported his usual unshaven face.

For the most part, he only granted a television interview to Katie Couric of NBC. However, Grisham's books sold whether he made a personal appearance or not. At Burke's in Memphis, people have waited in line all night or at least 6 or 7 hours before his arrival. Then, they developed a new system—only 250 people were allowed to come. They were to buy books first and buy a ticket. Even those appearances to favored bookstores have diminished, although he will pre-sign books for them.

When the former owners of Burke's Bookstore, the Beesons, first met John Grisham, they attended a book signing of *A Time to Kill* in Hernando. He was selling his books out of the back of his Volvo. Grisham gave the Beesons his book. They found him friendly and gracious. Once he became a regular at their Memphis store, he became part of their book-family. The staff and clients couldn't wait for him to come, and he enjoyed the rough and tumble of the camaraderie.

The Beesons and eventually the new owners placed an enormous billboard on top of their building that had a photo of Grisham's face and the words "Grisham's Coming" in large, bold letters, plus the dates of his arrival. Charlie, from a nearby restaurant, brought large helpings of barbecue to the signings. Grisham would drink Perrier water and eat the sandwiches throughout the penning of his name. Even those appearances have decreased.

During the autograph party for Grisham's fourth novel, *The Client,* he had to sign 2,000 copies of the book at Burke's. It took 13 and a half hours. His arm felt so tired, the Beesons soaked the arm in ice. After that experience, they changed their system for his signings…limiting them to just two hours.

Near Black Oak, Arkansas, where John spent the first six years of his life, is Blytheville. Here is another favorite independent bookstore of Grisham's, That Bookstore, owned by Mary Gay Shipley. It is off Main Street. The bookstore is long and narrow with creaky floorboards. At the back is a potbellied stove where soups, coffee, and tea are brewed. Sometimes, Grisham spent the whole day there. All the authors sign slatted, folding chairs. They are stacked on a shelf and brought down every time the authors come. Because John Grisham came almost every year to Blytheville, other authors would accept invitations to come even though the bookstore was in a rural, remote area.

Mary Gay Shipley, owner of That Bookstore in Blytheville, said to a reporter, "Sometimes I feel that Jesus could come back and sign the Gospels, and my customers would rather know about John Grisham's latest book. He has single-handedly made it really cool for lots of people to read. He's made a lot of people realize that reading can be fun and that's really important, not just for booksellers, but for the world."

According to the vice-president of merchandising for Barnes & Noble bookstore, "The first day his books are on sale, everyone is in the store buying the book. The Grisham name adds that 25% of customers who purchase a new Grisham hardcover and also purchase at least one other book at the same time. While we depend on bestsellers to make up only 3%-4% of our weekly sales, Grisham is wonderful because he brings people into the store to buy other books."

After his first two novels and the success of *The Firm* as a film, John Grisham was a rising star.

9

TWO HOME RUNS AND FIFTEEN MORE TO GO

The beginning of fame was at first sweet for John Grisham and his family. In 1991 Grisham told a variety of reporters, "Having a bestseller is so much fun. I don't think anybody's having more fun than I am." In 1992 he told another interviewer, "A lot of times I feel like it's happening to somebody else, but I'm philosophical about all this, in that five years from now or ten years from now things are not going to be as hot as they are now. Everything has X number of years to it, and I know that."

In his self-interview of 1993, Grisham spoke of his wildest dreams. "Every person who's ever written a novel dreams of bestsellers and fat royalty checks. Every kid playing Little League baseball dreams of hitting a grand slam to win the World Series. No difference."

When a reporter from *Christianity Today* interviewed Grisham in 1994, he asked Grisham about money and fame. Grisham replied, "It's unsettling. It's happened in two years, but we were comfortable before this happened. I had been practicing law for ten years and working very hard. So we were not going without anything. But you struggle when all this money is dropped in your lap; you ask, 'Why has it happened to me? What am I supposed to do with it?'"

In further reflection he said, "We've always had the attitude that fame is temporary. It's very much like the career of an athlete. There are some good years and some bad years, but one of these days it will be over, and we've always said that we hoped we would look back and say it was fun while it lasted, we kept our feet on the ground, we didn't change, and it's time to go on to something else."

The question was then posed to Grisham as to whether he ever asked himself, "Why me, God?"

He answered, "Yes, I used to ask all the time. I'm getting used to the success, but the questioning still hits occasionally.

I go for long walks in the woods a lot, and I ask myself if I'm handling it the way it ought to be handled. I don't know why it happened to me. God has a purpose for it. We are able to contribute an awful lot of money to his work, and maybe that's why. But I firmly believe it will be over one of these days…The books will stop selling for whatever reason. All this is temporary."

When Grisham was asked why his novels were so popular, he said, "One thing that helped is that the books are relatively clean, and when *The Firm* was published, a lot of people bought the book and realized they could give it to an older teenage son or daughter or to their parents. So the books were passed around. I hope it says something about our culture that you can be successful without succumbing to all the gratuitous sex and language that is so prevalent today. I have never been tempted to resort to gratuitous sex, profanity, or violence. I couldn't write a book that I would be embarrassed for my kids to read…Plus my mother would kill me."

Other writers have inspired John Grisham such as Graham Greene and Mark Twain. Of contemporary and competitive writers in the legal genre, he enjoys David Baldacci, Scott Turow, and Steve Martini. Grisham has said that he learned plotting through reading the works of Ken Follett, Robert Ludlum, John Le Carre, Thomas Harris, and Raymond Chandler. For his own personal pleasure, Grisham likes to read books about aviation, World War II, and baseball as he told a contestant winner on his web site.

But Grisham could not rest on the cushion of his success. He had to keep writing books. When *The Firm* grabbed the reading public with such intensity, Grisham's agent pushed him into writing his third novel at marathon speed.

With some projects in the past, Grisham has admitted to not finishing them. However, the book contracts give him a deadline and a goal. He told "Writer's Digest" in an interview, "When I have deadlines, it means I've promised things. So I know I've got to do it. *The Pelican Brief* was written in about 100 days. My publisher gives me a deadline for the first draft. That deadline goes up on the wall. Four to five months before that date, I kick into gear."

"When the deadline is on the wall—that's the term we use around the house; my kids know it…I'll write from 5 or 6 a.m. until noon. I average eight, nine, or ten pages of manuscript per day. That's a lot. I'll work six or seven hours, and get a bit more than a page an hour…Then usually, I'll go back at night and proof or edit a little bit."

"But even when I'm not writing, I'm always thinking about what comes next, the next scene. I do a lot of jogging to get away from the stress. When I'm jogging or fishing or bush-hogging, I'm still thinking about the next scene."

The Pelican Brief is about a female law student who writes a brief, depicting a conspiracy theory which points to the White House as responsible for assassinating two Supreme Court Justices. One justice is old and radical while the other is younger and a homosexual. When the brief gets into the hands of the FBI and the White House, the young woman's life is in danger. Her law professor is blown up in his car. She was supposed to be in the car, but they had an argument and she refused to ride in his car. Rumor has it that Grisham pretended the character of the law professor was one of his least favorite law professors at Ole Miss.

This is the first major role for a woman in Grisham's books. Perhaps she is modeled after Renee because the law student is tall and beautiful as well as brainy. In the movie, Denzel Washington plays the reporter, who helps and protects the female student, played by Julia Roberts.

John Grisham's own distrust of the FBI and CIA can be found over and over in his novels. Apparently his contact with agents through his law practice and in dealings his father had with them has made him very suspicious.

Because *The Pelican Brief* is set mainly in Louisiana, it has personal significance for Grisham because Grisham's father had worked on the canals and levees near Delhi, Louisiana. Even then, the oil companies were battling those groups interested in preserving wildlife—the pelicans. *The Pelican Brief* may have a concealed double meaning: the removal of two Supreme Court Justices through assassination; and the removal of pelicans in potential oil fields by extermination in real life.

When this third novel came out, the reviewers were critical. They thought the novel was a copycat of *The Firm*, except the leading character was female. They criticized the characters as being one-dimensional. The ending of *The Pelican Brief* was similar to *The Firm*. After the bright young female lawyer's conspiracy theory turns out to be correct, she negotiates with the FBI for money, a new identity, and safe flight to a new home...the Virgin Islands. Somehow the isolation of a bright young mind for a lifetime on an island, though romantic, seemed a waste.

Even the criticisms could not stop the tidal wave of buyers for the book. Doubleday printed 425,000, but that wasn't enough. The books were swept off the shelves. They did several more printing runs and by spring of 1993 there were 1.35 million hardback copies and 4.5 million paperback copies.

Ironically, a 3.7 million paperback edition of *A Time to Kill* was released at the same time as *The Pelican Brief.* The overload of Grisham books didn't seem to matter. Audiocassettes of his three books flooded the market, too. Grisham, Doubleday, and Dell were all happy.

But Grisham had to keep pumping out a new novel. He dipped deep into his memory for something new and something different. From his childhood Grisham remembered sneaking into the woods with his brother and smoking the butt ends of cigarettes. While they were engaged in this mischievous act, a car drove up close to them. Both boys were terrified. This little incident became the seed of an idea for novel number four, *The Client*.

Sensitive to criticism from book reviewers about the lack of character development in *The Firm* and *The Pelican Brief*, Grisham spent a little more time developing his main characters. In essence, the book is about an 11-year old boy, Mark Sway, and his younger brother who sneak into the woods to experiment with smoking cigarettes. Suddenly, a black car drives practically next to them. The boys hide and watch the driver try to kill himself by filling his car with carbon monoxide. The boy keeps removing the tube from the exhaust pipe to save the man. Finally, the man discovers him, grabs him, forces him in the car, and frightens him by threatening to shoot him. In a drunken stupor the man reveals where a politician was shot and buried. Then, the man commits suicide. The boy and the assassin of the politician are the only two who know this vital piece of information. Thus begins the chase of the FBI and the mobsters to get the information and do away with the boy.

The Client was published in March of 1993 and was turned into a movie in 1994, directed by Joel Schumacher. Actress Susan Sarandon played the boy's lawyer, Reggie Love (Grisham's second female lead in a book and movie).

Although both were successful, Grisham struck out with a number of reviewers, who accused the author of a flimsy plot. When asked if he thought an 11-year-old was that smart to hire a lawyer and outsmart the authorities, Grisham replied, "Sure. I'd think of my son who was nine and add two years." Readers still bought the book. The foreign rights to the book were sold in 36 languages as they were with *The Firm* and *The Pelican Brief*. All of his books were printed in paperback editions and sold millions.

Still stinging from the accusations of his books being too shallow, Grisham launched into a subject involving deep questions...the death penalty. His fifth novel would be titled *The Chamber*. The chamber would represent the death chamber. Before the book was written, the movie rights were sold to Universal Pictures. Ron Howard was hired to direct it.

Although Grisham has expressed his dislike for research, he dug into this question of the death penalty by reading books on the subject and going to Parchman, a facility in Mississippi for death-row prisoners. There he went into the gas chamber, sat in the chair, asking to be left alone in the chamber to know what it felt like.

"I talked to the guards and the administrators, and I talked to the inmates. It's a very dramatic thing to do, and it leaves a deep impression. You are just over-whelmed," said Grisham to a reporter on the Memphis Business Journal.

The Chamber has a complex plot. Two men were involved in bombing the offices of a Jewish lawyer who defended blacks in the 1960s. Unexpectedly twin toddlers were killed as well. Only one killer was caught and tried, but found innocent. Years later the case was reopened and that same man was sent to prison with only 30 days left before being executed. His grandson, a young attorney, offers to take the case for free. Despite his efforts, he wasn't able to gain life imprisonment for his grandfather.

The book has a less fragmented ending than some of the earlier ones. And Grisham tucked something personal into the text. The young attorney in the story goes to Mountain View, Arkansas, on the White River to gain some infor-mation from a retired FBI agent. This is the place where Grisham's parents have retired.

The same business reporter asked Grisham how he felt about capital punish-ment. "I was very much in favor of the death penalty before I started the book, but I'm now very ambivalent. I'm not comfortable discussing it," he replied.

Doubleday published the book in May of 1994 and the film came out in October of 1996. Again, the foreign rights were turned into 36 languages. *The Chamber* would become a movie in 1996, starring Chris O'Donnell, and was not received particularly well by the critics.

Grisham had to keep writing a novel a year. His sixth novel would touch on another sensitive subject—insurance companies that don't compensate the poor and helpless; and domestic abuse. This novel was called *The Rainmaker*. If a new, young attorney could bring a client, worth $20 million dollars, to his new law firm, he would be called a rainmaker. This almost happened to Rudy Baylor as a law student trying to help the elderly for free, but he didn't get the job and had to open his own office.

Instead, the young lawyer tries to help a poor family recover expenses for their son who is dying of leukemia. The insurance company tries to settle for a nomi-nal sum, but Rudy sues them for $50 million. He wins, but the insurance com-pany goes bankrupt. Rudy leaves Memphis and the law and decides to go somewhere to teach. He wins the girl that he had fallen in love with and she goes with him.

The ending of *The Rainmaker* is more realistic than some of Grisham's other novels. But Grisham's contempt for the law can be seen again and again. However, Grisham's dealings with an insurance company as a rookie lawyer himself gave him first-hand experience, which paralleled the main character's struggle with the insurance company in the novel. Grisham had to gather medical and further legal research to give this book authenticity.

In April 1995 Doubleday published *The Rainmaker* and in March of 1996 the paperback edition emerged. Famed movie director, Francis Ford Coppola, directed the film version, released in November 1997 by Paramount.

In 1995 Grisham's agent Jay Garon died from a heart attack. Saddened, Grisham had to find another agent to replace him. David Gernet, editor at Doubleday, had worked on all his books. Grisham turned to Gernert and asked him to become his agent. Gernert resigned from Doubleday and set up his own agency to help Grisham and other authors.

The death of Garon uncovered a huge scandal involving Grisham as the victim. In fact, Grisham discovered that Garon and his lawyer, Elliott Lefkowitz, had secretly stolen money from him. Like the skilled lawyer he had trained to be, Grisham took action and sued Garon's estate in 1996. Grisham claimed that excessive commissions from his books were funneled to Garon and Lefkowitz in secret payments. Garon's agency claimed that commissions would still be owed to them after Garon's death. Grisham asked the court to terminate the agency agreement at the time of Garon's death. The author also filed for damages and attorney fees. Garon hadn't bargained for an author with a legal background in which his embezzling would backfire. Grisham was someone not to be dismissed lightly—even after Garon's demise.

This case was launched only two months before Grisham's seventh novel, *The Runaway Jury,* hit the bookshelves in May 1996. This time Grisham attempted to tackle the issue of the tobacco companies and place a law suit in a suspenseful plot. Only a couple of years later in the American courts, the tobacco companies would be sued for causing lung cancer among those who smoked their product. Grisham's novel was timely. Again, he was striving to give depth to his thrillers and tackle current issues in a fictional form.

Essentially, the novel is about a professional juror who tries to manipulate the rest of the jury to his way of thinking. The ending has an unusual twist to it. The setting is on the Gulf Coast of Mississippi. Grisham used the research from a colleague in that area. The paperback edition appeared in February of 1997. Both editions, the hardback and paperback, stayed on *The New York Times* bestseller list between 24 and 26 weeks. Despite mixed reviews, readers were not slowing down in their purchase of Grisham books whether they were good, bad, or average.

The film adaptation of *Runaway Jury* was produced in October of 2003, starring Dustin Hoffman, Gene Hackman, and John Cusack.

Despite his aversion to life as a real lawyer, Grisham took a breather in 1996 to go back to court to represent the family of a client (pro-bono) over a railroad accident that pinned his client, a railroad brakeman, between two cars and killed him. Unsure as to his legal abilities after so long an absence, Grisham need not have worried. He won the case and $683,500 for his client's family.

In 1997 when Grisham wrote his eighth novel, *The Partner,* he drew upon his knowledge of Brazil. As a Baptist, John Grisham went with members of his church in Oxford down to Brazil to build churches and clinics for poor people along the Amazon River. From those experiences, he was able to use descriptions for a very effective opening to the novel, set in Brazil. A law partner from a firm in Biloxi, Mississippi, had stolen and hidden $90 million in Brazil. A deal to return the money is worked out. The partner gives his girl friend his share of the money and agrees to meet her in the south of France to get married and begin a new life. The woman takes the money and disappears. Again, Grisham provides a more satisfactory and realistic ending.

The Partner enjoyed 30 weeks on The New York Times bestseller list in hardcover and 20 weeks in paperback. Grisham decided not to sign over movie rights to Hollywood. In fact, he held back film rights on his future books for a time. The theory that the movies interfere with the sales of books is not true, according to the one of the former owners of Burke's bookstore in Memphis. She claims that the movies enhance the sales of all Grisham books. In the beginning Grisham didn't care what Hollywood did with translating his books into films. Now, he does. He demands much more control in casting and in overseeing that the film is true to the book.

For his ninth book Grisham would sacrifice suspense for another social issue…homelessness. His 1998 novel would be *The Street Lawyer.* This time the setting is in Washington, D.C., where homeless men sleep on the grate right outside the State Department. Grisham was given a guided tour of the area and the homeless shelters.

In true Grisham tradition, the opening of *The Street Lawyer* startles the reader. A Washington, D.C., black, homeless man takes over a prestigious law firm and holds the partners hostage until a SWAT team kills him. One of the attorneys is haunted by the whole episode. He gives up his job to take a less than half cut in pay to work on legal issues for the homeless. The lawyer plans to sue his old law firm. They cut a deal and the head partner, stirred by his conscience over the homeless, offers the skills of his firm to help the shelters a few hours a week.

The message of *The Street Lawyer* is a worthy one, but the drama and suspense are sacrificed to a wobbly plot structure. However, Grisham himself may have felt satisfaction as an author. But again, the sales soared and *The Street Lawyer* stayed on the New York Times bestseller list for 26 weeks.

In 1998 Grisham wrote an original screenplay, *The Gingerbread Man,* about a Georgia attorney who tries to help a woman in desperate trouble, which was caused by her father. Director Robert Altman took on the project with stars such as Robert Duvall, Kenneth Branaugh, Daryl Hannah, and Robert Downey, Jr. Despite the star power, the film was savaged by the critics and was not a box office hit. Grisham's tenth book in 1999, *The Testament,* was a fresh, new story and plot. The opening, almost always, is riveting. An elderly billionaire in a wheelchair writes his final will and then throws himself off a balcony to suicide. The last Will and Testament was intended to stop his greedy children from partaking in his millions. So, he leaves $11 billion dollars to an illegitimate daughter who is a missionary in Brazil. A drunken lawyer, who is twice divorced, is assigned to the case. His job is to find the daughter in the dense jungle of Brazil and tell her the news. Of course, he is met with disaster after disaster before he meets her. Finally, he finds her and she does not want the money (as the reader already suspects). Anyway, the lawyer undergoes a transformation or a spiritual conversion.

According to an interview with *Newsweek* magazine in February of 1999, Grisham had wanted to describe a full-blown spiritual conversion in the book, but his wife and editor objected. They prevailed. However, the whole book is a spiritual journey and poses questions about success, money, and true happiness. Because of his own missionary trips and work for the Baptist Church in Brazil, Grisham admits that Brazil provides him with a rich landscape for fiction.

With the opening of the millennium, Grisham hit the bookstores with a 2000 February book, called *The Brethren.* This is a title used by other authors such as Bob Woodward in profiling the members of the Supreme Court. Since there is no copyright on titles, anything is usable. Basically, the book describes the story of three imprisoned lawyers, who devise a scam to make hundreds of thousands of dollars by framing wealthy men in homosexual relationships. They stash away the money in a Caribbean island. When it gets close to a presidential candidate, the CIA gets involved.

Entertainment Weekly asked Grisham how he thought of the idea. "The idea came from a real scam that happened about 12 years ago. There was this guy in the Louisiana State Penitentiary in Angola—one of these criminal minds that can come up with wonderfully complicated ways to make money. He put ads in the gay magazines and blackmailed the guys who wrote back, like in the book. It was actually a very serious crime. I toned it down a bit, came up with the idea of the three judges, but it was basically very similar. And then I asked myself, Okay, who could they hook with this scam that would be very dangerous."

The opening of *The Brethren* is not a blockbuster like most of his other books. Usually Grisham grips the reader at the beginning and keeps the suspense going to the end. This one doesn't devour the reader until the last third of the book. It received mixed reviews, but climbed to the top of the bestseller list despite the flaws. Grisham has no dedication and list of acknowledgments, which may indicate his fatigue with writing thrillers.

However, in the *Oxford American* magazine, of which he was publisher, Grisham serialized in six parts his next book called *A Painted House*. With this book Grisham crossed over into the category of a serious southern writer. He wrote from the heart and he wrote what he knew—life as a poor boy growing up in Black Oak, Arkansas. Black Oak is the setting for the novel. The seven-year-old boy, Luke, is the main character and it is semi-autobiographical.

The Hallmark Hall of Fame presented a television version of *A Painted House* in April of 2003 to a favorable reception.

There are many autobiographical references for the author in the novel; especially the obsession with baseball. But the time of the novel is 1952 (Grisham was born in 1955) and in the story the boy is an only child (John was one of five children in his own family). Grisham did pick cotton for his Daddy on their land in Black Oak—that is one truth. The Grishams did live in a plank, unpainted house and they did go to the Baptist Church—more truths. The migrant workers for the cotton fields came from the Ozarks and from Mexico—yet another truth.

A Painted House is not written to formula as the legal thrillers are. The boy becomes a witness to a murder in a standoff between the Mexicans and the hill folks. What we do learn about John Grisham is that he is a skilled storyteller. His descriptions of Black Oak and southern food take us there to make the reader see and smell rural life in a little, itty-bitty town outside Jonesboro, Arkansas. Grisham even creates an innocent love interest between the boy and a 17-year-old female migrant worker. Grisham makes us imagine the blowing dust in a flat, dry Arkansas town until we visualize the balls of cotton running across the highways and falling into clumps in a ditch. The rain and floods that come unexpectedly capture the reader. His writing is clean, but colorful—not heavy-laden like William Faulkner's.

When asked about *A Painted House* by *Entertainment Weekly* in February 2000, Grisham responded, "It's a highly fictionalized childhood memoir of a month in the life of a seven-year-old kid, who is basically me. The setting is rural Arkansas in the early '50s. A place where my grandparents lived and where my parents lived, and where I was born and lived the first seven years of my life. Two or three of the people in the story actually lived, and some of the events actually happened. A lot of it is family stories, passed down over the decades. I've taken all of it and scrambled it up and just fictionalized the daylights out of it...and there isn't a single lawyer in it."

Grisham told another journalist, "It was inspired by my rural childhood in rural Arkansas. The setting is reasonably accurate, though historical accuracy should not be taken too seriously. One or two of these characters may actually have lived and breathed on this earth, though I know them only through family lore, which in my family is a most unreliable source. One or two of these events may indeed have taken place, though I've heard so many different versions of these events that I believe none of them myself."

The magazine also asked him if all the ideas for his books came from newspaper articles. "They drop in from all directions. Some gestate for years and some happen in a split second. They'll rattle around in my head for a while, and I'll catch myself mentally piecing it together. How do I suck the reader in, how do I maintain the narrative tension, how do I build up some type of exciting end? A lot of ideas don't work out. I have a lot of great setups that I can never finish. Right now I have about ten ideas I'm working out on paper. Some of those will work, some won't."

The serialized novel turned into book number twelve. The secret that the boy keeps after witnessing a murder is unburdened to the boy's grandfather towards the end. The ending, including a short epilogue, has greater realism than his other books. The plots and subplots are well drawn and hold the reader's interest throughout. Again, Grisham is writing what he knows and *A Painted House* (2001) has the same ring of truth to it that his first novel, *A Time to Kill,* has.

John Grisham's books took a new turn in the fall of 2001. Instead of one book a year, debuting early in February of every year, Grisham launched a second book in the autumn of 2001. This would happen in future years as well. Two books a year became somewhat of a Grisham standard. The February book would be a heavyweight and the second one would be a small, lightweight story. *Skipping Christmas* was the first in 2001. It is an original twist on the Christmas theme. A couple decides to skip the whole tradition of Christmas. They intend to scrap decorations on the outside of their home; scrap entertaining neighbors; scrap giving gifts. Instead, they sign up for a cruise. Everything backfires. The neighbors become hostile. Their daughter unexpectedly comes home for Christmas. She restores the whole spirit of Christmas, and the cruise goes out the window. Thus, Grisham writes a small classic for this time of year as his thirteenth book.

In 2004 *Skipping Christmas* was under consideration for a movie, but the title was in competition with a similar title. A new name had to be found if the project was to move ahead. It was changed to *Christmas with the Kranks,* starring Tim Allen and Jamie Lee Curtis.

Also in 2001, Grisham wrote and co-produced an original movie called *Mickey.* Producer Hugh Wilson joined him on this project. Both men lived in Charlottesville, Virginia. It was about Grisham's favorite topic—baseball. The plot revolved around a widowed father with a son who played a Little League pitcher. Unfortunately, the boy was about to turn thirteen...too old for Little League. The film starred Harry Connick, Jr. and was made for $6 million dollars and was 92 minutes long. The two producers put up their own money. However, they couldn't find a distributor and had to resort to their own marketing devices. In May of 2004 Grisham arranged for 18 screenings in the South and made personal appearances to promote the film.

As a Little League coach, Grisham has a strong philosophy. "Every kid plays in every game. In fact, our league has a mandatory play rule, and all coaches support it. I don't know much about winning. I ignore parents. If they gripe and complain, I invite them to take their precious bundle elsewhere."

By February 2002, Grisham produced another legal thriller called *The Summons.* His fourteenth book was considered very lightweight and almost two-dimensional without too many subplots to give the reader some grist. The plot was simplistic. A father, a retired judge in Clanton, Mississippi, sends a letter to his two sons, summoning them to the family home on a certain date. When they arrive, the judge is dead. The search for the murderer is not too well disguised, leaving the reader disappointed and wanting more.

About *The Summons,* Grisham has said, "I have not only returned to writing thrillers, I have returned to Ford County, Mississippi, for the first time since *A Time to Kill.* I enjoyed revisiting a place rich in colorful characters and dark family secrets."

With a touch of humor, John Grisham says in an AP interview regarding criticism about his books, "The worst letters come from retired high school English teachers. They will literally take a book and pick it to pieces and send me 14 pages of notes."

None of that seems to bother his readers. They buy his books, put him on the bestseller lists, and he laughs all the way to the bank! With more than 100 million books sold by 2004, Grisham readers were undeterred by bad reviews. Grisham is proudest of his success in foreign countries. Translations of his books in places like Paris and Milan have brought him enormous satisfaction.

Book number fifteen in 2003, *The King of Torts*, comes with a more compli-cated plot and more subplots. Obviously, from Grisham's own experience as a lawyer, he knows the millions of dollars that can be made by law firms that sue companies or the government over accidents of injury to persons by experiment-ing with drugs, which send people to mental institutions or to death. This is a more difficult read for the average person not familiar with this kind of legal greed. Grisham probably was motivated to expose such practices through the medium of fiction to send a message. A tentative love story underlies the major theme.

The second book in 2003 was *The Bleachers*, another small book that touched a universal chord with many readers. High school football was the setting for the story. Star players from fifteen years ago come back to Virginia to attend the funeral of their coach. In the bleachers they reminisce about those years of success and about their coach. Grisham probably modeled his coach after a composite of the coaches he knew in high school and college. He portrays the coach as a larger-than-life bull driver. The old players are now paunchy and not terribly successful, but still keep the high school memories alive. The protagonist even attempts to make amends to his high school sweetheart for dumping her for a sleazy girl. Even for non-football fans, this book has a moving ending.

Grisham came bounding into 2004 with a first rate blockbuster. *The Last Juror* established John Grisham as a southern writer of substance, going beyond the formula of a legal thriller. The author returns to the setting of Clanton, Mis-sissippi, which was so successful in *A Time to Kill*. In real life, this is the De Soto County courthouse in Hernando, Mississippi, where Grisham himself practiced in the courtroom. A young journalist buys the local newspaper and spices it up with graphic pictures of a local murder, splashed across the front page of the newspaper. A single mother of the 1970s is raped and murdered in front of her two, small children. She identifies her murderer as she draws her last breath. The son of a family Mafia is the killer. How to get a fair trial is at issue. After the life sentencing of the young man, he threatens to kill every juror.

The interesting part of this book is how Grisham expresses his opinions about the Vietnam War and about racial discrimination in the South before its gradual emergence into integration. The friendship that develops between a black family and this young journalist is beautifully drawn and touches the heart. There was a simple and perfect ending to the book. Grisham has honed his trade as a skilled writer. He does best when not writing to formula, but more from the heart.

An interesting fact about *The Last Juror* is that Grisham began the novel fifteen years ago and put it aside. At the start of his career, he wanted to write every other book about Ford County, but the publisher didn't see eye to eye with him on this idea. The right timing came in 2004. For the most part, the reviews have been full of praise.

Because of so much criticism over the years, Grisham has a critical view of book reviewers, "I have learned not to read reviews. Period. And I hate reviewers. All of them, or at least all but two or three. Life is much simpler ignoring reviews and the nasty people who write them. Critics should find meaningful work."

After that comment, the author of this biography will risk her own overview of Grisham's work thus far. From her point of view, Grisham's best books have been *A Time to Kill, A Painted House,* and *The Last Juror.* The characters in these books have been fleshed out to give the reader a real feeling of their personalities in a three-dimensional style. Each of these books has a soul.

In approaching nearly twenty years as an author, John Grisham has written 17 bestsellers that have made home runs on *The New York Times* bestseller list. What will his future be? Will he continue to write legal thrillers or more serious books or will he turn to something else?

10

LACK OF PRIVACY AND THE FUTURE

When the Grishams moved to Oxford, Mississippi, and built their dream house, they thought life couldn't be more perfect. Grisham built a baseball diamond on his land for his son. His own desire to teach Little League baseball was fulfilled. There was a tall wooden fence around his property for privacy, but the hilltop Victorian house could be seen from cars at every angle.

In this state of happiness John Grisham gave an interview to *People* magazine and said, "We wanted to build the home that the kids will come someday with their kids. We plan on living here forever. Ten years from now I plan to be sitting here, looking out over my land. I hope I'll be writing books, but if not, I'll be on my own pond fishing with my kids. I feel like the luckiest guy I know." One of Grisham's favorite pastimes was to climb on his bush-hogger and mow the acres of grass on his land.

These dreams were soon shattered. After two or three of his books and films became celebrated here and abroad, John Grisham's own celebrity grew with them. His youth, his handsome appearance, and his talent for writing what the general public wanted to read thrust him into the spotlight. He didn't like it and didn't want this kind of exposure either for himself or his family.

One of his best friends in Oxford is Billy Chadwick, who coaches tennis at Ole Miss. Chadwick (a younger look-a-like to movie star Wayne Rogers from the television series *M*A*S*H*) said, "John Grisham was in the Mississippi legislature and knew a zillion people. They all thought he was their best buddy. So when 30,000 to 40,000 people came to a football, baseball, or basketball game, the politicians used that opportunity to work the games for votes. When they came to Oxford, they would go up to John's house to talk and have him sign books."

"Because John Grisham was a celebrity," he continued, "he wasn't sure his children would be disciplined in the schools. He was afraid the children would be treated special because of his celebrity."

Oxford has always been on the tourist circuit because of the famous writer, William Faulkner. His white plantation home, Rowan Oak, is open to the public. Usually the busload of tourists would see Elvis Presley's Graceland on the outskirts of Memphis; drive down to Oxford to see the Faulkner homestead; and soon, the Grisham home and property became part of the circuit. The Grishams could see the buses slowly go past their land. Cameras were snapping from windows. If individual fans drove by, they would sometimes come up the winding drive and knock at the front door to ask for an autograph.

As these unannounced visits became more frequent, Renee, John, Ty, and Shea had some code words, which meant to get inside and hide as quickly as possible. The Grishams had no intention of leaving Oxford until something happened that upset them. They had stepped out onto their porch and suddenly discovered a couple standing in their cow pasture. They were getting married. That was the last straw. Their privacy was over.

The Grishams began to search for privacy in another state. Charlottesville, Virginia, was the place they found. Coincidentally, William Faulkner had also gone to Charlottesville from Oxford in 1962 to be near his daughter. There, the Grishams found a 204 year-old house on over 100 acres in Covesville, part of Albermarle County, and only 20 miles outside Charlottesville.

The new Grisham homestead was buried from public scrutiny. No one could find them. Among the rolling hills of Virginia and the stately horse farms, hidden behind white fences and giant trees, John and Renee found the perfect retreat. This time their house was set well back from the road, virtually invisible to curious fans.

Initially, the Grishams moved there in 1993 for a year, but they stayed because they achieved what they wanted—total privacy. John had a separate cottage where he could write his books every morning. There was another cottage for visitors, separate from their home. However, their rural setting has a swimming pool, tennis courts, a croquet court, horses, a housekeeper, a maintenance man, and a private jet. The jet picks up relatives and friends who come to visit, or Renee and her mother can fly off to Paris if they wish.

In a press conference Grisham said, "It is true I now spend most of my time in Virginia. We went for one year to hide and stayed another and another. My children are in school and we do enjoy it because of the privacy we receive. But Mississippi is still home. I still have a Mississippi driver's license. I still file state income tax in Mississippi. I'm still registered in Lafayette County to vote…I am very content to stay on the farm and write and coach Little League."

The one thing missing in the move to Virginia was a baseball field for his son and his Little League team. They had to travel 40 minutes to reach the nearest one. John Grisham soon fixed that. In 1995 he bought 109 acres for the Cove Creek Park. Here he built four regulation Little League baseball fields and two practice fields for 500 kids. Grisham would coach the Piedmont Little League Baseball Association, providing all the uniforms and equipment. Girls' softball teams would participate, too. Grisham would transport the team to Oxford for games or bring the Oxford team to Virginia. However, once his son graduated from high school, Grisham was less obsessed, but still active, with his volunteer work as coach and assistant coach. At the University of Virginia (where his son, Ty, played for two seasons), Grisham anonymously gave money to help build the $4 million new stadium for the Cavalier baseball team. John Grisham likes to be a quiet giver. However, he openly supported John Kerry's candidacy for the presidency in 2004.

Good friend Billy Chadwick said, "In Virginia John's virtually anonymous. If he went to live in Alabama or any other state, he'd be anonymous. If Stephen King came to live in Oxford, he would be anonymous. But because of John Grisham's legislative experience, he can't be anonymous in Mississippi."

Despite his move to Virginia, John Grisham keeps in close contact with his two universities in Mississippi and flies to both of them for football and baseball games. He will give speeches on the two campuses, refusing most other invitations.

Dr. Nancy Hargrove, who teaches 20th century American Literature at Mississippi State University and received a Grisham award, recalled those early visits to MSU, "When he first came here to speak, he seemed very uncomfortable. Now he is more at ease. After *A Time to Kill* had been published, maybe 20 people came to hear him. Several years later as he was beginning to become known, he came back and spoke and about 40 people attended. Then, of course, the last time he was here to speak more than 1,000 people attended."

Although Grisham has made millions from his books (probably $100 million by the year 1999), he and his wife Renee have been generous in sharing their wealth. To churches of all denominations, but particularly in Mississippi, they have contributed to specific needs and given amounts in the six figures. In Oxford, Grisham quietly gave $55,000 to have the two barns restored on William Faulkner's property.

Among many worthy causes, the Grishams have given to both of the Mississippi Universities from where John graduated. At the University of Mississippi in Oxford in 1993, John and Renee created two programs to bring emerging writer as well as famous writers to the campus.

The first program has brought one to three famous writers to the campus for brief visits each semester. They give public talks and meet privately with students. This is called The Visiting Writers Series.

Grisham supports a second program called The Emerging Southern Writers in Residence, which invites a writer for the entire fall semester. The selected writer teaches one course and is available to students for consultation. Grisham generously purchased a small house near the Faulkner homestead where the writer can live on a salary amounting to approximately $44,000. With any free time, the writer can work on his or her new writing projects.

When asked why he and his wife chose these two programs, John Grisham replied, "If there is one university that should have a strong writers program, it's the University of Mississippi. We wanted to enhance the strong literary atmosphere here by having many different kinds of authors come to the Oxford campus and also to nurture an environment, which might produce more writers. I remember how much I enjoyed it when Willie Morris brought writers like William Styron and George Plimpton and John Knowles to speak at Ole Miss while I was a law student."

At Mississippi State University in 1993 John and Renee established two awards: the Master Teachers and Faculty Excellence. The Master Teachers Award has a stipend of $3,000 a year for two years. Master teachers are supposed to serve as role models and mentors for their colleagues during the two year period. The Faculty Excellence Awards, which can be as many as five, carry a stipend of $2,000. That amount has increased and Grisham made it retroactive.

Every year since 1993 the University of Mississippi has held an Oxford Conference for the Book under the sponsorship of The Center for the Study of Southern Culture. In April of 1994, John Grisham and Stephen King appeared on the same panel to talk about writing. Wearing his trademark denim shirt and stroking his two-day growth beard, Grisham responded to the questions with humor in his deliberate Mississippi drawl. Wearing a William Faulkner tee shirt, the Maine writer King matched the Grisham humor in tight New England phrases. Both writers felt trapped by their long contracts to publishers and both were skittish about dealing with Hollywood. Yet, both agreed that they had fun in their chosen field as writers and felt they had a good life, except for the invasion of privacy.

Rarely did John Grisham write anything other than books. However, there was a literary magazine, created in 1992 as a place for southern literature that proved of interest to Grisham. A young man from northern California, Marc Smirnoff, was drawn to Oxford, Mississippi, and landed a job at Richard Howorth's Square Books. He became an instant Grisham fan. But he noticed what clients wanted to buy—works by southern writers. The idea for a magazine as a forum for new and established southern writers was his inspiration for "The Oxford American."

The tall, lean, handsome Smirnoff launched his first issue with a Grisham article—a satirical piece about the media. Smirnoff and Grisham had a tug of war over the editing. Smirnoff required many rewrites until it was acceptable. Grisham had respect for the young editor. Six months later Grisham asked Smirnoff to help him edit *The Client* and *The Chamber*. Grisham also expressed interest in a private stock offering of the magazine when Smirnoff decided to do it. Of course, Smirnoff wasn't making money with his sophisticated magazine, which only had a color cover until later. He could only pay $35 per article. Most writers wrote for free.

Finally, Smirnoff invited Grisham to become the magazine's publisher. Grisham was reluctant to accept. He knew that people would criticize him for striving to be in William Faulkner's league. Grisham decided to accept in order to help the magazine remain financially successful. The magazine still didn't made money, but they had 17,000 subscribers and an impressive color magazine. Smirnoff's goal was to reach a subscriber list of 50,000. Grisham was an occasional contributor. He became a major contributor in the year 2000 when *A Painted House* was serialized.

The magazine was sold and relocated to Little Rock, Arkansas, and stopped publication in July of 2003. But Smirnoff persuaded the University of Central Arkansas to buy it in May of 2004, retaining him as editor.

One of the most meaningful aspects of celebrity for the Grisham family is the John Grisham Room on the third floor of the new Mitchell Memorial Library at Mississippi State University. The university's dignitaries were on hand May 4, 1998 for the dedication of the room as they watched author Grisham cut the ribbon. The room is large and handsome with beautiful wood floors. Two seating areas, furnished in formal styles, are for visitors, receptions, and educational programs. Cabinets, holding all the Grisham books and posters in many languages, surround several pillars. Other display cases hold memorabilia from the early Grisham books, including letters from editors and agents.

Across the hall from the Grisham Room is the Special Collections Library, which holds all the papers from each of Grisham's books and from the papers related to his legislative experience. Most of these documents remain restricted to researchers and interested students. Newspaper clippings from 1989 to the present are readily available.

What John Grisham's future will be totally up to him. His contract with Doubleday, for whom he writes one book a year and sometimes, two a year, expired in 2004. The speculation is that he will renew with them. Grisham's life pattern has been fairly predictable. He tired of being a lawyer; he tired of being a politician; he may tire of being a fiction writer of legal thrillers or he may not. He has made all the money he could want. One theme that he has repeated to the press is a desire to help people; especially young people. Whether that will be through his mission work for his church or through something else is not clear. However, he has been writer-in-residence at the University of Virginia in Charlottesville, sharing his writing expertise with aspiring college students.

Grisham has offered advice to aspiring novelists. "Once you get the door open, you've got to have the drive to stay there. The smartest thing I ever did was write and publish the next book after *The Firm,* the year after. I've done it every year since then. Fifteen years ago I had it all planned, and thank goodness it didn't work. If you're sitting out there now with a nice, neat little outline for the next ten years, you'd better be careful. Life may have other plans. Life will present you with unexpected opportunities, and it will be up to you to take a chance, to be bold, to have faith and go for it. Life will also present you with bad luck and hardship, and maybe even tragedy, so get ready for it. It happens to everyone."

As a writer, Grisham may want to attempt more thoughtful pieces of fiction to place him solidly in a category of serious southern writers. He may want to combine these with his commercial thrillers. Whatever his choices, his seventeen plus books have compelled people, who never read or rarely read books, to venture into bookstores. These nonreaders eagerly await his books and sometimes wish he could produce more than two books a year. Few other authors can claim that kind of success.

And so, the man who struck out as a baseball player, hit more home runs on *The New York Times* bestseller list than any other popular writer.

BIBLIOGRAPHY

Books:

Contemporary Authors. Vol. 47, 1995, pp. 151-153.

Contemporary Literary Criticism. Vol. 84, 1995, pp. 189-201.

Current Biography Yearbook. 1993.

Grisham An Exhibition. University of Mississippi. August, 1994.

Author read all 17 of John Grisham's books.

Magazines:

Grisham, John. Publisher's note. *Oxford American.* February, 1995, p. 4.

Grisham, John. "The Birthday." *Oxford American.* March/April, 1995, pp. 60-63.

Grisham, John. "Unnatural Killers." *Oxford American.* Spring, 1996, pp. 2-5.

Hahn, Tina. "Sanctuary for the Soul." *Ole Miss Alumni Review.* Spring, 1998 pp. 24-26.

"Mississippi." Mississippi Division of Tourism. 1998.

Oxford American. "The Hollywood Question." Vol. 3, 1993, pp. 42-46.

Oxford American. "The Painted House." A six-part serialized novel during the year 2000.

Svetkey, Benjamin. "Making His Case." *Entertainment Weekly.* February 11, 2000. pp. 37-40.

Multimedia:

Couric, Katie. NBC television interview with John Grisham. February 2, 1999.

Oxford Conference at the University of Mississippi. "Surviving Success" with John Grisham and Stephen King at the Center for the Study of Southern Culture on April 10, 1994.

Newspapers:

Baswell, Allen. "Viewing the Grisham Room." *The Reflector.* September 29, 1998, p. 1B.

Grisham, John. "The John Grisham Interview." *U.S.A. Weekend.* July 2-4, 1993, pp. 4-6.

Lipe, Charles. Letter to the Editor. *Oxford Eagle.* October 23, 1998.

Howard, Edwin. *Memphis Business Journal.* April 25, 1994, pp. 37-42.

Street, Robin. "The Grisham Brief." *Writer's Digest.* July, 1993, pp. 32-34.

Toepfer, Susan. "Raising the bar." *People Weekly.* March 15, 1993, p. 1.

University News. "John, Renee Grisham Fund Two Programs." March 4, 1993.

Wible, Zac. "Grisham comes to give awards." *The Reflector.* September 18, 1998, p. 1A.

Wible, Zac. "A Time to Honor." *The Reflector.* September 29, 1998, p. 1A

Libraries:

Jonesboro, Arkansas, Public Library.

Mitchell Memorial Library: Special Collections at Mississippi State University.

Newspaper clippings from 1991–1998.

Richland Parish Library in Mississippi.

Ripley, Mississippi, Public Library.

Internet:

MSU website

Microsoft Internet Explorer under John Grisham.

CNN News

Page One Literary Newsletter

0-595-32283-2

Printed in the United States
22338LVS00006B/145-261

9 780595 322831